The

KERRY

Hospitality Guide

2001

GW00640801

*Kerry for lovers...
of the
Good Things in Life*

Georgina Campbell's Guides

Editor Georgina Campbell

Georgina Campbells Guides Ltd.,
PO Box 6173
Dublin 13
Ireland

website: www.ireland-guide.com
email: info@ireland-guide.com

Cover Photographs:
Looking towards Blasket Islands, Dingle, Co. Kerry
courtesy of Cork Kerry Tourism
Right to left:
Park Hotel Kenmare
Doyles Seafood Restaurant & Townhouse, Dingle
Aghadoe Heights Hotel, Killarney
Pony Trekking, courtesy of Cork Kerry Tourism
Sheen Falls Lodge, Kenmare
Climbers' Inn, Glencar

Design and artwork by The Design Station, Dublin
Printed in Ireland by Beta Print Ltd., Dublin

First published 2001 by Georgina Campbell's Guides Ltd.

ISBN: 1-903164-04-4

Foreword

by Dr. James McDaid T.D.,
Minister for Tourism, Sport and Recreation

I was delighted to be asked to provide a short greeting to the readers of Georgina Campbell's Kerry Hospitality Guide This is an objective, quality reference guide that will prove invaluable to many throughout the coming year.

As one of Ireland's leading food writers, Georgina Campbell clearly has a vision for the future of Irish food and a vital aspect of that future is recognition of regional strengths. As the county with the longest history of tourism in Ireland, Kerry has a leading role to play as a showcase for quality food production, fine food on the plate and genuine hospitality. Georgina Campbell's Kerry Hospitality Guide has sought out those individuals with a passion for perfection and commitment to excellence, making this an important publication that will lead many visitors to experience the very high quality of Kerry's finest establishments.

Quality, diversity and value are the hallmarks of the Irish dining and hospitality experience, from pubs to family-run restaurants, from hotels to gourmet establishments - and there's no better place to find these qualities than Kerry. This big-hearted county has restaurants of the first order, priced to suit every budget, from early-bird specials to extensive à la carte offerings - and a growing number of four and five-star hotels also provides for the demands of increasingly sophisticated and discerning visitors.

For the establishments recommended by this guide, inclusion is an accolade in itself and I congratulate all those who have been selected for these pages - and also the quality food producers who enable chefs, restaurateurs and hoteliers to identify local produce on their menus with pride.

With this publication, Georgina Campbell makes a crucial contribution to Kerry's tourism and hospitality industry. I am confident that Irish people and overseas visitors alike will find it to be a useful, highly-credible companion when visiting Ireland's longest established and, many would say, most beautiful holiday area.

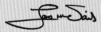

Dr. James McDaid, TD
Minister for Tourism, Sport and Recreation.

Prices and Opening Hours

PLEASE NOTE THAT PRICES AND OPENING HOURS MAY HAVE CHANGED SINCE THE GUIDE WENT TO PRESS. TIMES & PRICES ARE GIVEN AS A GUIDELINE ONLY AND SHOULD BE CHECKED BEFORE TRAVELLING OR WHEN MAKING A RESERVATION.

Any guideline prices given are based on high-season rates.

Acknowledgements

The publication of this guide would not have been possible without the support and encouragement of the Kerry County Tourism Committee and "A Taste of Kerry".

The contents of this book are believed to be correct at time of printing. Nevertheless, the publisher can accept no responsibility for errors or omissions or changes in the details given.

Contents

A Kerry

You are very welcome to Kerry, the HEART of Ireland and a golfers' paradise.

Kerry is situated in the beautiful SouthWest of Ireland with the most varied and spectacular scenery in the country, and yet only 50 minutes by air from Dublin (see page 14).

It is also an ideal cultural base with numerous archaeological and historical sites, some dating back to pre-Christian times and a wealth of traditional Irish language, folklore and song to experience. Kerry is home to Killarney's National Park, which boasts more trees than any other county - Kerry is indeed 'A Breath of Fresh Air'.

The Kerry Hospitality Guide introduces you to some of the culinary delights Kerry has to offer and the range of quality accommodation where traditional hospitality awaits you.

Kerry food producers are world renowned; this, combined with the artistry of some of Ireland's top chefs, makes dining in Kerry a memorable experience. Food is a major part of Kerry's culture. Visitors can see the fine rural setting that forms the basis of Kerry

Kathleen O'Regan-Sheppard

Kathleen O'Regan-Sheppard
Chairman, Kerry County Tourism Committee

Don MacNamara

Don MacNamara
Manager, "A Taste of Kerry"

Kerry is for lovers...

Welcome

food production, be it the beautiful fertile land, the cattle and sheep roaming the green fields and mountains, or the bountiful rivers and lakes.

But Kerry's culture is not simply about fine dining. It also has a host of other qualities valued by the discerning visitor, including outstanding accommodation, traditional Irish music, hill walking, mountain climbing, cycling, golf and a whole range of sporting opportunities. Kerry's wonderful scenery makes touring the Ring of Kerry, the Dingle Peninsula or Killarney's National Park/Lake and Mountain district an unforgettable experience. The heritage towns of Kenmare and Listowel have a special appeal of their own and festivals like The Rose of Tralee are renowned worldwide.

Most of all, perhaps, Kerry's culture is about the life and soul of its people. Kerry people are passionate people who invite you to share their passion for life.

Bíonn fáilte i gCiarraí i gcónaí (there is a welcome in Kerry always).

We invite you to 'Taste of Kerry'

Declan Murphy
Tourism Manager, South Kerry

Ogie Moran
Regional Manager, Shannon Development

of the good things in life!

A Taste of Kerry

Naturally

'A Taste of Kerry' is a county based food marketing company which promotes the range and quality of Kerry and Irish food products.

'A Taste of Kerry', through a number of activities, showcases the range of quality premium products available at a local and regional level.

Through its activities it works with some of the finest establishments in Kerry and beyond and 'A Taste of Kerry' is delighted to be associated with this guide to Kerry's Finest Places to Eat, Drink and Stay.

The quality of 'A Taste of Kerry' remains the very best that you can buy and enjoy... In Kerry... In Ireland... In the World.

'A Taste of Kerry'
FBD House, Ashe Street, Tralee, Co. Kerry.
Telephone 00 353 66 712 9155

Introduction

Welcome to the first ever independently assessed Kerry Hospitality Guide.

Kerry is a wonderful county: with great diversity and breathtaking contrasts, it really is a place apart - and a great choice for lovers of the good things in life, including fine accommodation and outstanding restaurants and pubs as well as many of the more obvious attractions, like spectacular scenery, Gaeltacht culture and outdoor activities such as golf, walking and fishing.

When visiting Ireland on business connected with the international chefs' organisation Euro-Toques some years ago, the great French chef, Paul Bocuse - perhaps the world's greatest living chef - recounted a very interesting story about Kerry and its food. He and those other great chefs, his friends the Troisgros brothers, used to come to Kerry on fishing holidays several decades ago. Having caught a fine salmon one day, they brought it back for their friend, that other great and famous chef, the Kerryman Ernie Evans, to cook for their dinner. They were, of course, used to pretty fancy fare in their multi-starred restaurants but Ernie Evans' wild Irish salmon - lightly poached with delicious curds between just-flaking flesh, and simply accompanied by boiled new potatoes freshly dug from the Kerry soil - was a revelation of flavour and texture: "And so," said Monsieur Bocuse with a Gallic flourish, "I learned to cook salmon in Ireland!" This little tale said a lot about the late great Ernie Evans, of course - but it also said a great deal about the importance of the wonder of really good produce and its true enjoyment through simple cooking.

May this guide lead you to the best kind of Kerry places, and may the experience of warm hospitality, great ingredients and simple cooking leave you with memories that last a lifetime.

Georgina Campbell.

Georgina Campbell,
Editor.

www.foodisland.com

Welcome to this very special part of Ireland, the Food Island.

Bord Bia, the Irish Food Board, has been associated with Georgina Campbell's Guides since their inception, as a means of highlighting the best food and drink Ireland has to offer visitors to Ireland - and Kerry, with its great traditions of farming and hospitality, plays an especially important role in this.

We are delighted to have had the opportunity to deepen and extend this involvement recently by introducing Feile Bia - a festival of food.

The Charter that participating establishments have to sign is printed on the page opposite. This is a serious commitment. Many of the restaurants involved in Feile Bia are sourcing foods from their locality. This sector is particularly vibrant and recent years have seen an upsurge in the number of innovative and high quality products available from Ireland. The great diversity and long farming traditions of Kerry provide a wealth of food which we hope will make enrich your dining experience when identified on menus as local produce.

I hope that wherever in Kerry this guide may take you, that you will enjoy great food, drink and company and that Kerry's flavours will stay with you long after your visit.

Michael Duffy

Irish Food Board

www.bordbia.ie

FÉILE BIA
CHARTER

Use local food and drink product

Look for assurances, as appropriate,
that products are produced under
the Bord Bia or other recognised
Quality Assurance Scheme

Develop dishes and menus to profile
local foods and artisan products

Where practical identify and name the
farmer/producer of ingredients used on the menu

A Taste of The Kingdom's Fine Fare

Farming and tourism are the twin pillars on which Kerry's prosperity rests, so it should come as no surprise that much of the fine fare presented to guests in the Kingdom's restaurants is locally produced. The rich diversity of produce showcased by the best chefs can also be seen on display at the **Listowel Food Fair**, which is held at a range of venues around the famous north Kerry town every November. Here, a cross-section of the producers, manufacturers, suppliers and distributors who come to show off their wares at the Listowel Food Fair demonstrates what may be an unexpectedly wide range of local produce.

Kerry meats such as lamb and beef are deservedly famous and feature on virtually every menu in the county, so visitors will be reassured to know that "A Taste of Kerry" promotes the quality and safety of selected foods, including meats, sourced within the county and the company's client base includes hotels, restaurants, butcher outlets and specialist food producers, so keep an eye out for their logo. Kerry's meat products are represented at the big end of the scale by the **Kerry Group**, who are based in Tralee and have many successful brands, including Denny (sponsors of a national Irish Breakfast Awards scheme). At the other end of the scale, the Weise family's company **Continental Sausage Ltd.**, at Fossa just outside Killarney, is a small family-run business renowned throughout the country for their home-made German-style salamis, hams and various sausages like bratwurst, knackwurst and pepperoni; a visit to their shop is a must, especially coming up to Christmas when they stock lots of delicious German specialities not usually available in Ireland.

Local seafood is de rigeur at restaurants everywhere in Kerry and there are many companies specialising in different aspects of the business. Paddy Oí Mahony, for example, operates **Iasc Ui Mhatuna Teo** at Ballyhea, near Dingle, where various white fish are processed. In summer he also supplies salmon, lobster, prawns, crabs and mussels to hotels and restaurants daily - and exports to Spain, Germany and France.

Like other parts of south-western Ireland, Kerry has more than its fair share of fine farmhouse cheeses: two to look out for are Wilma's Killorglin Farmhouse Cheese, a gouda style cheese made in four varieties (plain; garlic; cumin; or cloves) and available at different stages of maturation from 6 weeks when it is soft and mild, to over 12 months when it is mature. No additives or preservatives are used. Another is Sheila Broderick's **Kerry Farmhouse Cheese**, a cheddar style cheese made on the family farm near Listowel, using only milk from their own herd. It is also made in several varieties (natural; garlic; chives; nettle; hazelnut) and, like Killorglin, has won numerous awards.

The warm climate and fertile land of the south-west favours specialised seasonal farming for niche markets and a growing number of small farms are concentrating on organic production. **An Paircin** at Kilflynn, near Tralee, for example, produces organic vegetables and herbs from July to December and delivers to households who pay a flat rate for mixed boxes - a different kind of 'lucky dip' and one to get you out of the rut of supermarket predictability, where there are no seasons and everything is always available.

By contrast, chocolate-making is perhaps an unexpected strength of Irish artisan production - and first time visitors unfamiliar with Kerry's artisan products may be surprised to find that one of the country's most highly praised chocolatiers, **The Skelligs Chocolate Company**, is based in a remote location at Ballinskelligs, way out west beyond Caherciveen and Waterville. Although only in business since 1996, Michael and Amanda MacGabhann have already built up an international reputation - not only for exceptionally high quality (winning gold, silver and bronze at Fortnum & Mason's "Best of Ireland Awards") but also for unique packaging, which is designed to be original, beautiful and useful long after the chocolates have been eaten.

This is just the tip of the iceberg of specialist quality food production in Kerry - other examples include bakeries such as **O'Sullivans of Killorglin**, who supply a

wide range of home-baked products to discerning hotels and restaurants around the county; real old-fashioned ice cream such as **Mac's of Killarney**, made (along with a range of fresh fruit sorbets) by Denis and Catherine McMahon, with weekly deliveries in their own refrigerated van; and delicious jams, chutneys, relishes, mustards and oils, made by Eileen O'Brien and, as she uses as much organic an local produce as possible, marketed as **"Food on the Wild Side"**. Slainte!

Kerry to Dublin in
50 Minutes

Aer Arann Express Reservations
1890 462 726
www.aerarannexpress.com

KERRY TO DUBLIN

FLIGHT NO.	DEPARTURE	ARRIVAL	DAYS OF SERVICE M T W T F S S
RE 250	0615	0715	• • • • • • −
RE 252	0910	1010	• • • • • • •
RE 254	1405	1505	• • • • • • •

DUBLIN TO KERRY

FLIGHT NO.	DEPARTURE	ARRIVAL	DAYS OF SERVICE M T W T F S S
RE 251	0745	0845	• • • • • • •
RE 253	1240	1340	• • • • • • •
RE 257	2210	2310	• • • • • − •

*Extra flights may be available in summer season.
Please phone for information.*

aer arann
express
your regional airline

Ballybunion

You don't have to be a total golf enthusiast to get full enjoyment from Ballybunion, but it helps...

In the mists of time, the full Irish name of this clifftop resort in North Kerry was Baile an Bhuinneanaigh - the townland of the Bunyans or Bunions. The beachside cliffs provided natural fortresses near the entrance to the Shannon Estuary, and a castle was built.

By the 20th Century, the beaches were appreciated for their leisure qualities, and it became a popular resort for traditional family seaside holidays. The renowned International Bachelor Festival at the end of June dates from that period.

But Ballybunion's best times were yet to come. South of the little town, there is one of the finest formations of sand dunes in all Europe. It was a golfing heaven, and the links course was much appreciated by discerning sportsmen.

A fine new clubhouse was built, and a second course was created to add to the perfection of this paradise. Ballybunion had arrived. When Bill Clinton was nearing the end of his final term as President of the United States, he is said to have confided in Taoiseach Bertie Ahern that his real dream retirement job would be as a Greenkeeper at Ballybunion.

RADIO KERRY

your voice in the kingdom · 97FM · guth na ríochta

fabulous fun

music and dance

sporting passion

**on the crest
of a wave**

and MORE!

For the best of Kerry Life
tune into Radio Kerry

BROADCASTING DAILY ON

96.2FM ~ Tralee & South & West Kerry

96.6FM ~ Killarney, 97FM ~ South Kerry & 97.6FM ~ North Kerry.

RADIO KERRY

• Tralee • Killarney • Cahersiveen •

Telephone: 066 71 23666   email: requests@radiokerry.ie

or visit our web site - www.radiokerry.ie

BALLYBUNION GUESTHOUSE/RESTAURANT/BAR

Harty-Costello Townhouse, Bar & Restaurant

Main Street Ballybunion Co Kerry
Tel: 068 27129 Fax: 068 27489
email: hartycostello@eircom.net

Although styled a townhouse in the contemporary mode, Davnet and Jackie Hourigan's welcoming town centre establishment is really an inn, encompassing all the elements of hospitality within its neatly painted and flower bedecked yellow walls, albeit at different times of day. Eight spacious, well-maintained en-suite bedrooms have not only television, direct dial phones, tea & coffee-making facilities and hair dryer, but also comfortable chairs - and curtains thoughtfully fitted with blackout linings to keep out intrusively early summer light. There's also a pleasant lounging area between the accommodation and the evening restaurant (also on the first floor) and a choice of no less than three bars in which to unwind. Seafood is the speciality in the restaurant, where both table d'hôte and à la carte menus are offered, complemented by an extensive wine list. It all adds up to a relaxing and hospitable base for a golfing holiday, or for touring the south-west.

Children welcome (under 10s free in parents' room). No pets. No private parking. 8 bedrooms, all no-smoking. B&B £45 pps (single £55). Table d'hôte dinner from £16.95.

Closed 30 October-1 April.

Amex, MasterCard, Visa.

Directions: On the right of the main street, heading towards the sea.

17

BALLYBUNION
BAR/ACCOMMODATION

Iragh Tí Connor

Main Street Ballybunion Co Kerry
Tel: 068 27112 Fax 068 27787

The name, which translates as "the inheritance of O'Connor", says
it all: what John and Joan and Joan O'Connor inherited was a 19th
century pub with potential and, thanks to their scrupulous
attention to detail when planning and sourcing materials like real
slates and wooden windows for its transformation, their inheritance
has now been transformed into a fine establishment with 17
exceptionally large en-suite bedrooms, including three junior suites.
All rooms have been carefully refurbished and furnished with
antiques to complement the convenience of satellite television,
direct dial phones and generous bathrooms with cast-iron tubs and
power showers - and many rooms even have working fireplaces,
where fires can be lit on request. Public areas, which include the
original public bar, a lounge bar and a fine dining restaurant with a
baby grand to add to the atmosphere, are also generous in scale,
and furnished with style and individuality. Golfing holidays are a
serious attraction here and Iragh Tí Connor is fast establishing a
reputation as one of the best places to stay on the discerning
golfers' circuits.

Children welcome. No Pets. Own parking. 17 bedrooms, 10 no-
smoking. B&B £60pps, single £90. Dinner à la carte.

Closed 24-26 December

Amex, MasterCard,Visa.

Directions: On the left as you come into the main street from
Listowel.

BALLYBUNION   GUESTHOUSE

Teach de Broc Country House

Links Road Ballybunion Co Kerry
Tel: 068 27581 Fax: 068 27919
email: teachdebroc@eircom.net

Just across the road from the practice ground and a couple of minutes' walk to the first tee, this is a dream of a place for golfers - but you don't even have to play golf to appreciate this understandably popular guesthouse, as Aoife and Seamus Brock's exceptional hospitality and care is even more attractive that the location. Their ten en-suite bedrooms include six executive rooms and one for wheelchair users, and offer all the comforts, including direct dial phones, TV and tea/coffee-making in all rooms. Recent extensions and refurbishments include a new dining room and an extra four deluxe rooms, plus the upgrading of existing rooms and, as the commitment is to constant improvement, standards continue to rise each year. But, however comfortable and well-located this outstanding guesthouse may be, it's the laid-back and genuinely hospitable atmosphere that really gets them coming back for more - they can even offer a choice of breakfast, including freshly-baked scones, from 6 am.

Wine licence. Not suitable for children. Own parking. 10 bedrooms, all no-smoking B&B £40-55pps, single £60. Wheelchair friendly.

Open all year.

MasterCard, Visa.

Directions: Directly opposite Ballybunion golf club.

Photo - View of Valentia Island from the Caherciveen Car Ferry.

Caherciveen

Cradled in the estuary of the Valentia River, Caherciveen provides a special sense of interaction between mountain and sea. In times past, its relative isolation at the distant end of the Iveragh Peninsula was an economic drawback. But growing prosperity has given the town fresh vitality, with urban regeneration being matched by the redevelopment of the harbour and its new marina.

Set in spectacularly beautiful scenery, you can learn of the Caherciveen area's attractions in the Tourist Office, which is in the Heritage Centre in the former police barracks beside the harbour - a building so dramatic in appearance that you'll accept the local story that the plans for a fort on the Northwest Frontier of Imperial India were sent to West Kerry by mistake.

Nearby Valentia Island is famed for its links with the earliest Transatlantic telegraph cables, and its exceptionally mild climate. The island can be accessed by car ferry from Reenard Point near Caherciveen across to Knightstown. But despite the regular frequency of the ferry, the island still retains a genuine away-from-it-all atmosphere. This is if anything emphasised by the famous sub-tropical gardens at Glanleam House in its spectacular setting above the sea.

CAHERCIVEEN   RESTAURANT

Brennan's Restaurant

12 Main Street Caherciveen Co Kerry
Tel: 066 947 2021 Fax: 066 947 2914
email: brenrest@iol.ie

Since Conor and Teresa Brennan's well-appointed restaurant first opened in 1993, they have earned a reputation as the area's leading fine dining establishment and opened a second dining room on the first floor (available for private groups of up to 20). Conor takes pride in using the best of local ingredients and serving them imaginatively but without overdressing, so dishes based on fresh seafood like Valentia scallops, Atlantic prawns, crabmeat, wild salmon, hake, turbot - and meats, including local mountain lamb - are contemporary in style, but not slavishly fashionable. Specialities like Caherciveen black pudding with caramelised shallots & a balsamic vinegar dressing or a parcel of three Irish farmhouse cheeses, baked and served melting over steamed asparagus tips with truffle oil indicate the style.

Home-baked breads and desserts are equally important and they operate a deservedly popular early dinner (5.30-7; £17), and a wide-ranging à la carte until 10 o'clock every evening in summer. A thoughtfully constructed wine list includes a good choice of half bottles.

Children welcome. Carpark nearby.

Closed 24-26 December;
also Monday-Wednesday from 1 November-15 March.

Amex, Diners, MasterCard, Visa.

Directions: On right in main street, approaching from Killarney.

CAHERCIVEEN PUB

O'Neills "The Point Bar"

Renard Point Caherciveen Co Kerry
Tel/Fax: 066 947 2165

Michael and Bridie O'Neill's immaculate pub has been in the family
for 150 years, and has been renovated in true character by the
present owners. It's very handy if you're travelling to or from
Valentia Island by ferry and it's worth timing your journey to sample
their super fresh seafood, served daily during the summer (except
Sunday lunchtime). The menu covers everything from a whole
range of salads and open sandwiches on brown bread – fresh and
smoked wild salmon, smoked mackerel, crabmeat, crab claws – to
hot dishes like deep-fried squid and a couple of hake and monkfish
dishes with garlic and olive oil. There's even lobster (market price)
and, although price increases have been inevitable due to less
plentiful fish stocks, everything remains as reasonably priced as
possible. Not very suitable for children. Wheelchair accessible. Own
parking.

Bar open all year (except 25 December & Good Friday). Phone ahead
to check opening times off season.

Food served in season only, ie April-October: Lunch Monday-
Saturday, dinner daily; closed Sunday lunch).

No credit cards.

Directions: Beside the Valentia Island car ferry (operates April-
September).

CAHERCIVEEN   BAR/RESTAURANT

QC's Char-Grill Bar & Restaurant

3 Main Street Caherciveen Co Kerry
Tel: 066 947 2244 email: acooke@oceanfree.net

Kate and Andrew Cooke officially opened QC's in June 2000 although, mainly due to the style and sensitivity with which they've renovated this old building, it already feels as if it's always been there. Special features include a big eighteenth century fireplace in the original stone wall of the bar (a cosy place to be on chilly days) and there's a locally crafted bar counter made of Irish oak that's over a hundred years old, plus numerous nautical antiques and pictures of local interest which all contribute to the character. More surprising, perhaps, is a pleasing Spanish influence. Local meats and fish feature - the fish is supplied by the family company, Quinlan's Kerry Fish at Renard Point - and, as a charcoal grill from the Basque region is a major feature in the kitchen, chargrills, with lots of olive oil and garlic, are typical of the style. Spanish omelette is, of course, another speciality (and very good it is too) and the wine list is almost exclusively Spanish. Children welcome. Toilets wheelchair accessible. Carpark nearby.

Food served Monday-Saturday 12.30-3 & 6.30-9.30 (Sunday from 5.30).

Closed 25 December, Good Friday. No lunch on Sunday.

MasterCard, Visa (minimum transaction £20).

Directions: Centre of Caherciveen, on right heading towards Killarney.

Caherdaniel

Although the most famous name associated with the Caherdaniel neighbourhood is Daniel O'Connell the Liberator (1775-1846), the "Daniel" of Caherdaniel was a pre-Christian chieftain called Donal whose stronghold, Cathair Donall or Donal's Stone Fort, is still to be found near the tiny village.

But it is the O'Connell house of Derrynane Abbey, the centrepiece of Derrynane National Park, which provides the focal point for an area which is enchanting in its mixture of gold and silver beaches, dense woodland, salt marshes, rocky islands, brooding mountains, and the ever-present sea.

Here, at a distance from the centres of power in Dublin and London, the O'Connell family preserved the ancient lifestyle of the Gaelic chieftains. But when a spokesman was needed for the dispossessed Irish people, it was from Derrynane that Daniel O'Connell emerged onto the wider world stage, prepared if need be to travel all the way to parliament in London for an eloquent presentation of the case for Emancipation.

The journey required 46 changes of horses, and sometimes took as long as 10 days. Yet always, whenever possible, he would return to Derrynane to restore his energies. Visit this wondrous place, and you will see why.

CAHERDANIEL   HOTEL/RESTAURANT

Derrynane Hotel

Caherdaniel Ring of Kerry
Tel: 066 947 5136 Fax: 066 947 5160

In a superb location on the seaward side of the Ring of Kerry road, this unassuming 1960s-style hotel enjoys stunning views and has access through informal gardens to the beach below. Although quite modest, the 74 en-suite rooms are very comfortable, the food is good and, under the excellent management of Mary O'Connor and her well-trained staff, this hospitable, family-friendly place provides a welcome home from home for many a contented guest. The bar and restaurant look over a heated outdoor swimming pool towards the sea and the best of local ingredients are used in imaginative food (including a 4-course Table d'Hôte dinner, £25). Salads and sandwiches available in the bar all day make this a place to consider planning a lunch stop on the Ring of Kerry. Outdoor pursuits of every kind are a big attraction, notably walking, fishing and watersports - and tuition is available for a wide range of activities, including golf, horseriding, canoeing, sailing, diving and windsurfing. Pets permitted by arrangement. No-smoking restaurant; air conditioning. Ample parking.

B&B £45pps, single £60.

Closed mid October-mid April.

Amex, Diners, MasterCard, Visa.

Directions: Midway between Sneem and Waterville on Ring of Kerry.

Photo - The Dingle Way, Camp

Camp

With its strategic location on the main northern approaches to the Dingle Peninsula, you could be forgiven for thinking that this tiny village gets its name from some ancient military encampment. But the word Camp comes from the Irish An Cam - The Hollow - indicating the valley which leads to the upland route past the Slieve Mish mountains to Anascaul, and then on to Dingle itself.

Travelling from Tralee, Camp is the gateway to the west, to Dingle and beyond. You can go directly over the mountains, or else take the coastal route past Castlegregory and above Brandon Bay, until the mountains are crossed by the impressive Connor Pass.

But instead of travelling on, there's much to be found in the Camp and Castlegregory area itself. Beaches abound, and the long sandy peninsula running from Castlegregory down to the Maharees, dividing Brandon Bay from Tralee Bay, is a delightful away-from-it-all sort of place, perfect for that holiday with a difference, while anyone with a taste for windsurfing is in paradise.

CAMP   PUB/RESTAURANT

Ashes Restaurant and Bar

Camp Tralee Co Kerry
Tel: 066 713 0133

This fine old pub has the genuine ambience born of 200 years of hospitality in one family. It's a delightful place, full of real character and a sense of shared pleasure in the delight shown by visitors. Chef/joint proprietor Rory Duffin takes pride in sourcing local ingredients for seasonal menus that include organic vegetables and herbs from their own garden in dishes that range from the traditional (steaks various ways), through numerous classical seafood dishes (Atlantic salmon bonne femme, baked monkfish & crab mornay) to more contemporary fare such as vegetarian couscous and polenta or smoked chicken and lemon pesto salad. Winter fare is restricted to an à la carte dinner menu, but the bonus is an opportunity to enjoy game in season - and a free low-season taxi service within a 20-mile radius, which takes in both Tralee and Dingle.

Bar food in summer, 12.30-7 (Sun to 8); Dinner all year 6-10; à la carte.

Closed 25 December & Good Friday. Phone to check opening times off season.

Amex, Diners, MasterCard, Visa.

Directions: On the main Tralee-Annascaul-Dingle road, 10 miles from Tralee.

CAMP   GUESTHOUSE

Barnagh Bridge Country Guesthouse

Cappaclough East Camp Tralee Co Kerry
Tel: 066 713 0145 Fax: 066 713 0299
email: bbguest@eircom.net

Attractive and comfortable, Heather Williams' unusual architect-designed guesthouse is tucked neatly into the hillside overlooking Tralee Bay, between the mountains and the sea. The five individually furnished guest bedrooms all have en-suite shower rooms and decor themed on local wild flowers. While good dinners are easy to find nearby, Heather's breakfasts are a speciality and guests can drink in the view of Tralee Bay from the dining roomwhile doing justice to – fresh juices, newly baked breads and scones, locally made preserves, and Dingle smoked salmon and scrambled eggs or a traditional fry (in addition to daily specials such as kippers or French toast). The stylishly decorated guest drawing room opens onto a patio overlooking the Maharees islands and their spectacular sunsets; the latest improvement planned is a conservatory, to extend the reception area and dining room - and maximise still further on the wonderful view. Garden, fishing, walking. Not suitable for children under 10. No pets. 5 rooms (all non-smoking). B&B £25 pps, single £35.

Closed 1 November-1 March .

Amex MasterCard, Visa.

Directions: Take the N86 Dingle road from Tralee; after 9 miles, take the Connor Pass/Castlegregory road R560; guesthouse is 1 mile on the left.

The Cottage Restaurant

Camp Tralee Co Kerry
Tel: 066 713 0022

Although newly built, both the design and materials of Frank & Gretta Wyles' bright, airy restaurant are in the local idiom so it fits in remarkably well already and will mature gracefully. It is a welcome addition to the local dining scene, especially because it's an all-year enterprise and, in high season, they're open over the middle of the day and have an outdoor seating area with tables and parasols. Seafood is a speciality (there are always daily specials) and also steaks, various ways; vegetarian dishes, such as goats cheese tartlet with a roasted red pepper & rosemary, are always on the main menu. Local ingredients feature in both contemporary international dishes like sweet chilli crab cakes with a smoked garlic & lime leaf dipping sauce, Thai vegetable curry and more traditional fare such as west coast chowder or rack of lamb with roasted vegetables, herb mash. Service is pleasant and prices reasonable (Dinner Menu £15.95; à la carte available lunch & dinner. Ample parking; children welcome. Wine licence.

Open all year. D 6-10 daily, L Sun 12-3.30 (daily 12-4 in July & August).

Amex, MasterCard, Visa.

Directions: On the Tralee-Castlegregory-Conor Pass-Dingle road (9 miles from Tralee).

Caragh Lake

Caragh Lake is a wonderful surprise. Travelling westward from Killorglin towards Glenbeigh and Caherciveen, there's more than enough spectacular scenery to be going along with. On the left, the majestic MacGillycuddy's Reeks unfold in all their glory. Ahead, the splendid peaks above Caherciveen dominate the skyline. On the right, there's a hint of the sparkling waters of Dingle Bay sweeping in to meet the beaches of Cromane, Inch and Rossbeigh.

Yet before you've reached Glenbeigh, a discreet road sign will tell you that Caragh is nearby. A short drive across flat country, and suddenly it appears, a jewel set between the mountains, a gem of a lake.

Caragh Lake is renowned for its trout and salmon fishing. But you don't need to be a fisherman to get full enjoyment from this exquisite place. For it is almost mystical in its profound sense of peace. Around Caragh, the worries of the world melt away. And the houses and hotels which look over its waters are in keeping with the mood and style of the lake. It has a wonderfully remote atmosphere, yet it is within easy reach of the other attractions of the Ring of Kerry.

CARAGH LAKE   COUNTRY HOUSE/RESTAURANT

Caragh Lodge

Caragh Lake Co Kerry
Tel: 066 976 9115 Fax: 066 976 9316 email: caraghl@iol.ie

Mary Gaunt's lovely Victorian house and gardens is an idyllic place, enjoying views of Ireland's highest mountains, the MacGillycuddy Reeks, and with salmon and trout fishing, boating and swimming all available at the bottom of the garden. The house – which is elegantly furnished with antiques but not too formal – makes a cool, restful retreat and the 15 bedrooms, which are all sumptuously furnished and have lovely bathrooms, include some recently added garden rooms with wonderful views and their own sitting room, complete with open log fire. Mary has a real love of cooking and baking is a particular strength, seen in delicious home-baked breads, baked desserts and treats for afternoon tea that includes recipes handed down through her family. At dinner, in the elegant dining room overlooking the lake, local produce takes pride of place and often includes freshly caught seafood, possibly even wild salmon from Caragh Lake, Kerry lamb and home-grown vegetables.

Children over 12 welcome. No pets. 15 Rooms (8 executive). B&B £62.50 pps, single £85, service included. D £33, 7-8.30; non-residents welcome by reservation. Licensed.

Closed mid October-mid April.

Amex, Diners, MasterCard, Visa.

Directions: From Killorglin on N70, Glenbeigh direction, take second road signed Caragh Lake; at end of road go left again. The house is on the right.

CARAGH LAKE   HOTEL

Hotel Ard-na-Sidhe

Caragh Lake Nr Killorglin Co Kerry
Tel: 066 976 9105 Fax: 066 976 9282
email: sales@kih.liebherr.com

Peace and tranquillity are the key characteristics of this romantic Elizabethan style retreat set in award-winning gardens and woodland in a breathtakingly beautiful mountain location overlooking Caragh Lake. More like a country house than an hotel in atmosphere, it was built by an English lady who called it the "House of the Fairies" and is still classically furnished in a soothing country house style, with open fires and chintzes - and, appropriately, now operates under the caring eye of general manager Kathleen Dowling. Luxurious antique-filled day rooms provide plenty of lounging space for quiet indoor relaxation and there's a terrace for fine weather – all with wonderful views. The 19 spacious and elegantly furnished bedrooms are shared between the main house and the garden house (some with private patios). The beautifully appointed restaurant specialises in international cuisine based on local specialities (Table d'Hôte dinner, £29; 7-8.30). Dooks, Waterville, Killeen and Mahony's Point golf courses are all within easy reach and leisure facilities at the sister establishments Hotel Europe and Dunloe Castle are available to guests. 24 hr room service. Not very suitable for children, although cots are available. No pets. 19 rooms (5 superior 2 shower only).

B&B £75pps, single £130, service included.

Closed 1 October-1 May. Restaurant closed Sunday.

Amex, Diners, MasterCard, Visa.

Directions: Off N70 Ring of Kerry road. signed 5 Km west of Killorglin.

Blaise na Ríochta!

Corca Dhuibhne agus Uíbh Ráthach

A search for Ireland's culture and heritage, peace and tranquillity, stunning scenery or holiday activities must inevitably bring you to the Gaeltacht.

Here the Irish language is an everyday community language for many of the inhabitants, reflecting a rich Gaelic heritage...

...a heritage of hospitality, great music, song and dance.

The Gaeltacht areas of Kerry lie at the tip of the Corca Dhuibhne and Uíbh Ráthach Peninsulas, two great fingers of land carved out by the great Atlantic Ocean.

Piled high with majestic mountains and fringed with quiet unpolluted beaches this colourful holiday destination is a haven for walkers, golfers, surfers, sailors, sightseers and deep-sea fishermen not to mention the best restaurants, pubs, music and a range of quality accommodation to suit all budgets.

Éire i mbláth a maitheasa !

Why not visit our website and see for yourself at **www.gaelsaoire.ie**

For more holiday information on the Gaeltacht areas contact Gaelsaoire at:

Freephone Ireland:	1800 621 600
Freephone UK:	0800 7835708
International:	+353 66 9152423
Fax:	+353 66 9152429
Email:	info@gaelsaoire.ie

GaelSaoire
SCÍTH SA GHAELTACHT
HOLIDAYS IN IRELAND'S GAELTACHT

Dingle

Dingle is Ireland's Atlantic port par excellence. Set on the edge of mountains, it interacts enthusiastically with the Western Ocean. Its fishing boats do business on great waters. And its marina is the most westerly in all Europe, attracting leisure sailors to some of the most spectacular seascapes in the world.

Dingle's lively interaction with the sea is personified by the port's most famous character, Fungie the Dolphin. Fungie has been part of Dingle life since 1984. Far from being a visitor, he is now the town's leading citizen. But although his playful antics in the approaches to the harbour are a continuing delight, don't think for a moment that this is some kind of tame nautical pet, for he is a superbly free creature of the ocean.

The port is fascinating in its own right. Strategically located at the end of the Dingle Peninsula, it has ancient links with sea trade routes along Europe's Atlantic seaboard. Thus although it is a small and compact town, it's a big-hearted place. And they know a thing or two about hospitality and living well. The standard and variety of cuisine in Dingle is simply astonishing, while it reputedly has fifty-two pubs, one for each week of the year, and every one with its own individual character.

A glance at the map might suggest that Dingle's location would give a sense of isolation. But once there, you'll soon realise that Dingle is so strong in its own sense of identity that it is readily seen as the hub in an enchanting world of its own.

Within the town there's much of interest, particularly Mara Beo, Dingle's Oceanworld exhibition, an informative introduction to the area's magnificently varied marine life. But equally, there's the shore life of a people who find themselves in a natural fortress. Thus the Dingle region has some of the most vibrant Gaeltacht areas, where the ancient Irish language lives on in a lively modern society.

And always, there's the timeless view to the west, to the Atlantic and the majestic Blasket Islands thrusting through its restless waters. The Blasket Centre at Dunquin celebrates the extraordinary way of life of those storm-battered islands, where in times past the people produced their individualistic literature in this region where evidence of ancient history abounds in the midst of bustling contemporary life in a large and peaceful landscape.

DINGLE   GUESTHOUSE
Bambury's Guest House

Mail Road Dingle Co Kerry
Tel: 066 915 1244 Fax: 066 915 1786
email: bamburysguesthouse@eircom.net

Jimmy and Bernie Bambury have been running their purpose-built guesthouse just a couple of minutes walk from the centre of Dingle for over a decade now and, for many returning guests, it has become a home from home. Their 12 spacious bedrooms - which vary in size and outlook and include doubles, twins and triples plus three suitable for wheelchair users - all have en-suite showers, tea/coffee trays, phone, satellite TV, hair dryer and complimentary mineral water and there's a comfortable lounge for guests' use. Griddle cakes with fresh fruit and honey are a speciality at breakfast - and vegetarian breakfasts are offered by arrangement. It's a good base for enjoying the many activities in the area and reduced green fees can be arranged on local golf courses. Not suitable for children under 4. No pets. Wheelchair access. Ample private parking. 12 rooms (all no smoking)

B&B £30 pps, single £45.

Open all year.

MasterCard, Visa.

Directions: On N86, on the left after the Shell garage on entering Dingle.

DINGLE

Benners Hotel

Main Street Dingle Co Kerry
Tel: 066 915 1638 Fax: 066 915 1412
email: benners@eircom.net

Right in the middle of Dingle, this 300 year old hotel has recently undergone major refurbishment and now provides a unique combination of traditional charm and contemporary comfort. Public areas include a streetside bar which gets lively at night and has more character than expected of an hotel (food available 6.30-9.30pm daily) and a large, bright, dining room towards the back of the building. But it is the addition of spacious new bedrooms at the back that has most improved the hotel. Bedrooms in the older part of the hotel have considerable charm and are furnished with antiques - some have four-poster beds - but the new bedrooms away from the road (and the bar) are quieter and more spacious. Rooms include four junior suites and two suitable for wheelchair users; all are en-suite and well-equipped, with television, direct dial phone, tea/coffee making facilities and hair dryer. Lift. Private parking. Children welcome (under 4s free in parents' room, cot available without charge). Pets permitted by arrangement. 52 rooms.

B&B £70 pps, single £85.

Closed 25 December.

Amex, Diners, MasterCard, Visa.

Directions: In centre of town, beside Lord Baker's.

DINGLE   GUESTHOUSE

Captains House

The Mall Dingle Co Kerry
Tel: 066 915 1531 Fax: 066 915 1079
email: captigh@eircom.net

Named after a Captain Tom Williams, who first took lodgers here in
1886, it seems appropriate that this charming guesthouse is
approached via a little bridge over the Mall river - and equally
appropriate that Jim Milhench, who took over the property with his
wife Mary in the late 80s, should also be a retired sea captain. They
renovated the house and furnished it with the antiques and curios
collected by Jim on his voyages, creating as relaxed and hospitable
a place as could be wished for. The age and nature of the building -
which extends into the next door premises - has created a
charmingly higgledy-piggledy arrangement of rooms that vary
considerably, but all have comfort (orthodpaedic beds, phones,
satelllite TV, hospitality trays, plenty of hot water) as well as
character. A welcoming turf fire in the reception area encourages
guests to linger over tea, or with a book, and breakfast - which is a
very special feature of a stay here - is served in the conservatory,
overlooking a lovely garden. Not suitable for children. No pets.

9 rooms (all no smoking, 7 shower only).

B&B £30 pps, single £35.

Closed 1 December-16 March.

Amex, MasterCard, Visa.

Directions: Turn right at town entrance roundabout; 100 yards on
the left.

DINGLE   RESTAURANT

The Chart House Restaurant

The Mall Dingle Co Kerry
Tel/Fax: 066 915 2255

Although traditional in appearance with its sturdy stone walls and colourful half door, Jim McCarthy's Chart House is very much a restaurant of our times, where informality and multi-cultural food work together to make dining out relaxed and accessible - and it's now firmly established as one of the most popular eating places in the area. While they are international in inspiration, menus are based on seasonal local ingredients - so, perhaps, Annascaul black pudding and apples may be spiced with ginger, wrapped in filo pastry and served in a bacon jus, or local steamed mussels could be served provençale with a hint of chili. Themes from closer to home could include spring cabbage accompanying a roulade of pork fillet with apricot and bacon stuffing - and Irish cheeses are offered with a glass of vintage port. The wine list has helpful tasting notes as well as country of origin and vintages - and, of course, Chateau MacCarthy is a best-seller. No smoking area, air conditioning. Dinner 6.30-10; à la carte.

Closed Tuesdays & 8 January -11 February.

MasterCard, Visa.

Directions: On the left at the first roundabout as you approach the town.

DINGLE   GUESTHOUSE

Cleevaun

Lady's Cross Milltown Dingle Co Kerry
Tel: 066 915 1108 Fax: 066 915 2228
email: cleevaun@iol.ie

Set in an acre of landscaped gardens overlooking Dingle Bay,
Charlotte and Sean Cluskey's well-run, recently renovated
guesthouse just outside the town is near enough to Dingle to be
handy and far enough away to enjoy the peace that the peninsula
promises - and make a good base for outdoor activities like walking
or pony trekking. Charlotte offers a cup of tea or coffee and a slice
of home-made porter cake to welcome guests on arrival, providing
an ideal opportunity to slow down, get your bearings and enjoy the
magnificent view. Furnishing throughout is in a pleasant country
pine style and bedrooms, which are all non-smoking, have good
facilities and are well organised, with quality beds, well-finished en-
suite bathrooms. TV, direct-dial phones and tea/coffee making
facilities; one bedroom even has a separate dressing room.
Charlotte's breakfasts – served in a large south-facing dining room
overlooking the sea – are a speciality, so plan your day to allow time
for a leisurely start. 9 Rooms (all no smoking, 1 shower-only).

B&B £32, single £55

Closed mid-November-mid-March.

MasterCard, Visa

Directions: Just outside the town, on the Slea Head/Ventry scenic
route R559.

DINGLE   HOTEL

Dingle Skellig Hotel

Dingle Co Kerry
Tel: 066 915 0200 Fax: 066 915 1501 email: dsk@iol.ie

A shoreside location within easy walking distance of the town, excellent facilities and a friendly laid-back atmosphere are among the reasons this modest-looking but well-run 1960s hotel has won many friends over the years. It is a particularly family-friendly place, with organised entertainment for children and a fine leisure centre. Roomy public areas are comfortably furnished with a fair degree of style - the tone is set in the large high-ceilinged foyer - and good use is made of sea views throughout, especially in the conservatory Coastguard Restaurant, which has special anti-glare glass. Bedrooms, which include three suites and 40 executive rooms, have been recently refurbished and are all fairly spacious, with compact bathrooms. In summer, the "Dingle Day Cabaret" offers evening entertainment through traditional Irish music, song and dance - and the hotel also has good conference and business meeting facilities, which are popular off-season.

Children under 3 free in parents' bedrooms; cots available; crèche, playroom, children's playground. Parking. 116 rooms (10 no-smoking).

B&B £85 pps, single £102

Closed Christmas week and 8 January- 8 March.

Amex, Diners, MasterCard, Visa.

Directions: On the sea side of the road as you approach Dingle from Tralee.

Doyle's Seafood Bar & Townhouse

John Street Dingle Co Kerry
Tel: 066 915 1174   Fax: 066 915 1816
email:cdoyles@iol.ie

For many regular visitors Doyle's is synonymous with Dingle, as it was the first serious restaurant in the area and attracted a loyal following over several decades. Currently in the good hands of Sean and Charlotte Cluskey (who also run Cleevaun guesthouse just outside the town), it has changed very little over the years - its flagstone floors and old furniture give the restaurant lots of character and local seafood has always been the main attraction. Lobster, selected from a tank in the bar, is a speciality. But there are also other choices, such as duo of Kerry mountain lamb (roast rack and leg with braised puy lentils, roast garlic & thyme jus) and traditional beef & Guinness stew - and vegetarians are well looked after too. Puddings arecomfortingly traditional or you can finish with farmhouse cheeses from the Munster region. The accommodation is of a high standard and includes a residents' sitting room as well as eight spacious bedrooms with well-designed en-suite bathrooms and antique furniture. No-smoking area & air conditioning in restaurant.

Dinner only, Monday-Saturday 6-10. A la carte.

B&B £42 pps, single £78.

Closed Mid November-mid February.

Diners, MasterCard, Visa.

Directions: on entering Dingle, turn right onto The Mall at roundabout, then right onto John Street.

DINGLE   GUESTHOUSE

Greenmount House

Gortonora Dingle Co Kerry
Tel: 066 915 1414 Fax: 066 915 1974
email: mary@greenmounthouse.com

Quietly located on the hillside, with views of the mountains across
the bay, John and Mary Curran's fine guesthouse is just five minutes
walk from the town centre and it's an exceptionally comfortable
and hospitable place to stay. Well-appointed bedrooms are shared
between those in the original house, which are furnished to a high
standard although smaller than the newer junior suites which have
generous seating areas and good amenities, including fridges as
well as tea/coffee-making trays, phone and TV (and their own
entrance and balcony). There's also a comfortable residents' sitting
room and a conservatory overlooking the harbour, where
exceptional breakfasts are served. They currently hold the Munster
title in the Denny Irish Breakfast Awards: an extensive buffet - fruits,
juices, yogurts, cheeses, freshly baked breads, home-made
preserves - is matched by an equally extensive choice of hot dishes,
including the traditional full Irish breakfast, smoked and fresh fish
and much more besides. Just remember this is not the place to skip
breakfast. Not suitable for children under 8. No pets. Own parking.
12 rooms (all no smoking);

B&B 45 pps, single £45.

Closed 10-27 December.

MasterCard, Visa.

Directions: Turn right and right again on entering Dingle.

DINGLE   GUESTHOUSE

Heaton's House

The Wood Dingle Co Kerry
Tel: 066 915 2288 Fax: 066 915 2324
email: heatons@iol.ie

Although it's just five minutes' walk from the town, Cameron and
Nuala Heaton's fine new purpose-built guesthouse is set in well-
maintained gardens just across the road from the water and it's
beyond the hustle and bustle of the busy streets. An impressive
foyer-lounge area sets the tone on arrival and spacious bedrooms,
which include four junior suites, confirm first impressions: all have
phones, TV and hospitality trays and are finished to a very high
standard with lovely bathrooms (with both pressure shower and
bath). Getting guests off to a good start each day is a point of
honour and breakfast includes " Heaton's Breakfast Treat (porridge
served with a topping of Drambuie and brown sugar and cream), an
extensive buffet (everything from fresh juices to cold meats and
Irish cheeses) and a full hot breakfast menu including several fish
choices. 16 rooms (all no smoking).

B&B £40 pps, single £65.

Closed 23-26 December.

Mastercard, Visa.

Directions: About 700 yards beyond the marina, on the west side of
town.

DINGLE

Lord Baker's Seafood Restaurant & Bar

Main Street Dingle Co Kerry
Tel: 066 915 1277 Fax: 066 915 2174

Believed to be the oldest pub in Dingle, this business was established in 1890 by a popular businessman called Tom Baker; a colourful orator, member of Kerry County Council and a director of the Tralee-Dingle Railway, he was known locally as "Lord Baker" and is now immortalised in John Moriarty's excellent pub and restaurant. A welcoming turf fire burns in the front bar, where bar food such as chowder and home-baked bread or crab claws in garlic butter is served. At the back, there's a more formal restaurant (and, beyond it, a walled garden). Seafood stars, as it does everywhere in the area, but there's also a good choice of other dishes – local lamb, of course, also beef, chicken and local duckling – all well-cooked and served in an atmosphere of great hospitality. Sunday lunch In the restaurant is particularly popular (booking strongly advised); on other days the lunchtime bar menu, plus daily specials, can be taken in the restaurant.

Open daily 12.30-2.15, 6-9.45. Set menus & à la carte. No smoking area. Toilets wheelchair accessible.

Closed 24-25 December & Good Friday.

Amex, Diners, MasterCard, Visa.

Directions: Town centre, on the main street.

DINGLE   GUESTHOUSE

Milltown House

Dingle Co Kerry
Tel: 066 915 1372 Fax: 066 915 1095
email: milltown@indigo.ie

The Kerry family's beautifully located guesthouse on the western side of Dingle, is set in immaculate gardens running down to the water's edge and enjoys lovely views of the harbour and distant mountains. Day rooms include an informal reception room, a comfortably furnished sitting room with an open turf fire and a conservatory breakfast room overlooking the garden, where tables and chairs are set up on the lawn in fine weather. Breakfast is quite an event, offering everything from fresh juices and fruit, through cold meats and cheeses, freshly baked breads and an extensive cooked breakfast menu. Although dinner is not served, a light menu is available in the conservatory (or room service, if preferred) from noon to 7 pm and there is a wine licence. The ten bedrooms – all very comfortable and thoughtfully furnished with bath and shower, phone, TV and tea/coffee making facilities - include three junior suites, two with private patios and one suitable for wheelchair users. Film buffs may be interested to know that Robery Mitchum spent a year here with his family when Ryan's Daughter was being filmed in the 1960s.

10 rooms (all no smoking). Not suitable for children under 10. No pets.

B&B £42 pps. single £65

Closed 23-27 December. Amex, MasterCard, Visa.

Directions: West through Dingle town, left at roundabout then next left.

DINGLE　　　　　　　　　　　　　　　　　GUESTHOUSE

Pax House

Upper John Street Dingle Co Kerry
Tel: 066 915 1518 Fax: 066 915 2461
email: paxhouse@iol.ie

The view from this modern house may well be the finest in the area – and, thanks to the exceptional hospitality and high standards of the owners, Joan Brosnan and Ron Wright, it is also one of the most comfortable and relaxing places to stay. Thoughtfully furnished bedrooms are well-equipped (with fridges, as well as TV, phone and tea/coffee facilities) and have well-finished bathrooms. Recent renovations and refurbishments have resulted in two suites with their own terraces where guests can lounge around and enjoy that stupendous view - and also a change in furnishing style, which is now daringly bright and fresh. Breakfast is a major event (you will notice that there is great competition in this area in and around Dingle) featuring fresh Dingle Bay seafood as well as an exceptional range of meats and cheeses, all served in a newly opened dining conservatory overlooking the bay. Garden. Children welcome. Pets permitted by arrangement. Rooms 13 (all no-smoking, 3 shower only).

B&B £35 pps, single £35

Closed December & January

MasterCard, Visa.

Directions: Half a mile outside Dingle; turn off at sign on N86.

DINGLE, AT VENTRY   RESTAURANT

The Skipper

Ventry Dingle Peninsula Co Kerry
Tel: 066 915 9900 Fax: 066 915 9994

Genuine French cooking and charming service at realistic prices are
hardly to be expected in this remote area, so Michel and Cathy
Chauvet's smashing little two-storey restaurant on the Slea Head
drive is all the more welcome. Seafood stars - traditional Breton
seafood soup with croûtons and crabmeat gratin are
mouthwatering examples, and there is much else beside including
lobster - good value and unusually priced by the 100g/^{1}/$_4$ lb, which
is practical. Or what about an omelette as only the French can make
them? Other French classics like confit of duck Périgord style sit
easily alongside more dishes more familiar to Irish tastes, like
steaks and Irish stew. It's worth venturing out of Dingle, or planning
your trip to Slea Head around mealtimes here if you can, as they
serve lunch (12-3.30) and dinner (5.30-10) daily in summer. Own
parking. Children welcome. Early Set Dinner about £10, 6-7.30 only,
otherwise à la carte.

Closed early November-mid March.

MasterCard, Visa.

Directions: On Slea Head road, 5 miles out of Dingle.

Photo - Walkers at Glencar

Glencar

Nestling in its valley on the western flank of Carrauntuohill, the sheltered nature of Glencar is emphasised by the ruggedness of its surroundings. Atop MacGillycuddy's Reeks, Carrauntuohill is Ireland's highest mountain, and many an international climbing career has begun in Glencar. But you don't need to be a mountaineer, nor even a hillwalker, to appreciate this neighbourhood with its classic Kerry mixture of purple peaks soaring above green valleys and dark woodland. It is tough country, with determined folk wresting a living from sheep-farming.

But the challenging nature of the environment creates a special sense of community among the people who live here, together with those who visit it regularly with a proper sense of appreciation. It is in the shelter of Glencar that you most readily realise that there's more to Kerry than elegant scenery. And at the busiest holiday periods, journeys which start and finish in Glencar will show you that there's always an uncrowded Kerry of little roads and secret places and quietly majestic vistas, for those who know how to seek it out.

GLENCAR   FOOD & ACCOMMODATION

The Climbers' Inn

Glencar Killarney Co Kerry
Tel: 066 976 0101 Fax: 066 976 0104
email: climbers@iol.ie

Ireland's oldest established walking and climbing inn (1875) is now run by the fourth generation, Johnny and Anne Walsh, who offer every comfort for the traveller, whether arriving on foot, on horseback or, more prosaically, by car. Accommodation is budget (hostel) or bed & breakfast (rooms with en-suite showers), all recently refurbished, functional and spotlessly clean. Wholesome home-cooked dinners, prepared by a guest chef from a different country each season, are served in the dining area of a bar reminiscent of alpine inns; the style varies but menus are based on local ingredients and aim to satisfy hearty mountain appetites with big soups, home-baked brown bread and main courses which include Kerry mountain lamb, wild venison or salmon (with plenty of wholesome vegetables and a good pudding). Bar food daily (12 noon–6 pm) in summer; barbecues with live music, Sundays in late July-mid August (3-7 pm). Not suitable for children under 10. Pets permitted. 8 rooms (all shower only & no-smoking).

B&B about £25 pps, single £30 (high season). Dinner about £15.

Closed November-March.

Amex, Diners, MasterCard, Visa.

Directions: From the Ring of Kerry, take the Glencar road from Killorglin; after 9 miles, look for Climbers Inn signs.

Kenmare

Kenmare is generous in its offerings, not least in having two names for the price of one. Officially, the Irish one is Neidin, the "Little Nest", which well describes this snug location where the Roughty River meets the sea in a sheltered place a whole world away from the rugged Atlantic of West Kerry.

However, the name Kenmare itself derives from Ceann Mara, the "Head of the Sea". And the estuary becomes so narrow that it is traditionally known as the Kenmare River, though increasingly you'll hear it referred to as Kenmare Bay.

But whichever name you support, there's universal agreement on one topic. The setting of Kenmare utterly beatiful, and blessed with a mild climate. So this compact little town seldom experiences frost, even if the mountains which soar above it are snow-capped in winter.

Ancient monuments indicate a long history of civilised living. There were well-organised small communities in Kenmare more than 3,000 years ago. Then, in the time of the Gaelic chieftains, the O'Sullivans and the McCarthys held sway, and in 1261, Finin McCarthy stopped the Anglo-Norman advance at the Battle of Callan a few miles up the Roughty Valley near Kilgarvan, a village which continues today as a focal point for Kerry's independent outlook.

Kenmare itself was first put on the maps by Sir William Petty in 1670. Putting things on maps or in documents was Petty's speciality, and he did it so efficiently that the English government rewarded him with 3,500 acres of confiscated land in the Kenmare region. He set about re-organising his new estate with the planned

Photo - Old Kenmare Road

township of Kenmare at its heart. But he had only a few years to enjoy it - he died in 1687. And he was a hard act to follow - his descendants and successors did not always fulfill his hopes of prosperity for the region, while the ebb and flow of national life saw the dispossessed Irish people maintaining an invincible presence.

Thus today's Kenmare really came into being with the new prosperity of tourism and improved commerce in the latter years of the 19th Century. That prosperity waxed and waned in the 20th Century. But by the 1980s, Kenmare was increasingly recognised as a place for the discerning visitor, with world class hotels, a growing reputation as a centre of gourmet excellence, and the very best of hospitality.

KENMARE, AT MOLL'S GAP RESTAURANT

Avoca Handweavers

Moll's Gap Kenmare Co Kerry
Tel: 064 34720 Fax: 064 35742

High up at a famous viewing point on the Ring of Kerry, this outpost of the renowned County Wicklow weaving company sells its fine range of clothing and crafts - and offers wholesome, home-made fare to sustain the weary sightseer. Avoca Handweavers claim, with justification, that this store is the finest craft shop you will experience on your journey around the Ring of Kerry - and that they serve the best country cooking in the area. In summer, freshly cooked food is served all day, seven days a week (9.30-5, Sunday to 5.30).

Parking. No-smoking area. Toilets wheelchair accessible.

Closed 10 November -12 March.

Amex, Diners, MasterCard, Visa.

Directions: On Ring of Kerry, 14 miles from Killarney, 6 from Kenmare at famous panoramic crossroads.

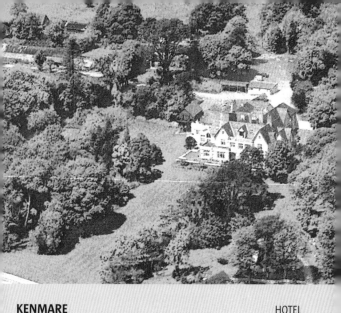

KENMARE   HOTEL

Dromquinna Manor

Blackwater Bridge PO Kenmare Co Kerry
Tel: 064 41657 Fax: 064 41791
email: dromquinna@tinet.ie

Set well back from the road, beyond a long tree-lined avenue, this mid-19th century manor enjoys an idyllic location in 40 acres of wooded grounds, with three quarters of a mile of sheltered south-facing sea frontage. The hotel has a number of unusual features including a romantic tree house (a 2-bedroom suite with four-poster and balcony, 15ft up a tree), a safe little sandy beach (beside the informal Boat House Bistro and marina) and a 34ft Nelson Sport Angler with professional skipper for fishing parties and scenic cruises. The interior of the hotel features an original oak-panelled Great Hall, a traditional drawing room complete with concert grand piano, a panelled bar, pool room and table tennis room. Bedrooms are all individually decorated to specific themes, with good bathrooms; a new ground floor suite is wheelchair friendly and an 18-room annexe includes family rooms. The hotel is understandably popular for weddings. Children welcome (playroom, playground). Tennis. Boating. Pets permitted. 48 Rooms (1 suite, 2 mini-suites, 2 shower only)

B&B about £45 pps, single £65.

Closed 31 October-17 March.

Amex, Diners, MasterCard, Visa.

Directions: 3 miles outside Kenmare on the Sneem road.

KENMARE   RESTAURANT

An Leath Phingin

35 Main Street Kenmare Co Kerry
Tel: 064 41559

As the ground floor is cosy in a traditional Irish way, visitors may be surprised to find that Cornelius Guerin's long-established restaurant specialises in northern Italian food. All is revealed as soon as the menu appears, however, or when going up to the first floor which is more stylish and arty, with Italian posters. Cornelius takes pride in sourcing the best of local ingredients - organic green salads from Billy Clifford, Kenmare smoked salmon for risotto, meats from the local "A Taste of Kerry" butcher - and interpreting Italian dishes with a certain amount of artistic chef's licence, which should not be seen as a criticism, as this is passionate cooking, well-executed and none the worse for some untraditional twists. Choices range from old favourites like salad Caprese, through home-made pork sausages flavoured with fennel and bruschetta, to a range of interesting home-made pastas (tortellini, perhaps, with spinach, ricotta and parmesan), risotto (typically with smoked salmon) and half a dozen pizzas. Reasonable prices (main courses in the £10-£13 region) and friendly, helpful service add to the enduring appeal of this attractive restaurant.Dinner,Thursday-Monday. A la carte.

Closed Wednesdays and 15 November-15 December.

MasterCard, Visa.

Directions: Town centre, next to "Treats" food & wine shop.

KENMARE   RESTAURANT

The Lime Tree

Shelburne Street Kenmare Co Kerry
Tel: 064 41225/42434 Fax: 064 41839
email: benchmark@iol.ie

In an attractive cut stone building built well back from the road in 1832, Tony and Alex Daly's hospitable restaurant has an open log fire, exposed stone walls, original wall panelling and a minstrels' gallery (making an upper eating area and showcase for local artists), which all make for a characterful interior. Seasonal menus always offer daily specials, including several imaginative vegetarian options such as Brutus Salad (a variation on the classic Caesar salad) and main courses like millefeuille of goat's cheese with house marinated peppers. Cooking is very sound and local produce – Sneem black pudding, local free-range duck and Kerry lamb (oven-roasted, with sweet mint pesto perhaps) – is highly valued; local seafood such as Killmacallogue mussels appear in delicious specialities like seafood potpourri "en papillotte". Finish, perhaps, with a traditional pudding like warm blackberry and pear fruit crumble. A warm welcome and caring service add greatly to the enjoyment of the dining experience. Wheelchair accessible. No-smoking area. No children after 7 pm.. Dinner daily 6.30-10; à la carte.

Closed November-March.

MasterCard, Visa.

Directions: Next to The Park Hotel Kenmare.

KENMARE COUNTRY HOUSE

Muxnaw Lodge

Castletownbere Road Kenmare Co Kerry
Tel: 064 41252

Situated just across the bridge and within walking distance from town, Hannah Boland's wonderfully cosy and homely house was built in 1801 and enjoys spectacular views across Kenmare Bay. Disregard any potholes in the rather steep driveway or a few cobwebs around the door - this is very much a home where you can relax in the TV lounge or outside in the large garden and you can even play tennis on an all-weather court. Tranquil bedrooms are individually furnished with free-standing period pieces and pleasant fabrics in a genuinely homely country house style; all the rooms are no-smoking and en-suite, with cleverly hidden tea/coffee-making facilities. Dinner is available if notice is given by noon – a typical dinner cooked in and on the Aga might be carrot soup, oven-baked salmon and apple pie, but guests are always asked beforehand what they like. 5 Rooms (all no-smoking).

B&B £24. Dinner £16.

Closed 25 December

No credit cards

Directions: First right towards Bantry after the double-arched bridge.

KENMARE   RESTAURANT

Packie's

Henry Street Kenmare Co Kerry
Tel: 064 41508 Fax: 064 42135

Tom and Maura Foley's buzzy little restaurant is stylish but
unpretentious, with small tables and a big heart. Great local
ingredients, especially organic produce and seafood, mingle with
imports from sunnier climes and, in Maura's skilful hands, result in
imaginative Ireland-meets-the-Med food that is memorable for its
simplicity and intense flavouring. First impressions are of world
cuisine and there's a clear awareness of international trends, but
the cooking here is far above the influence of fashion. Maura
modestly describes her food as "simple, with an emphasis on local
ingredients" but what makes it special is her sure judgment of
complementary food combinations, many of them traditional and
that is why they have lasted - crab cake with tartare sauce, rack of
lamb with rosemary and garlic sauce for example. Red onion and
caper salsa may sound like an exotic accompaniment for wild
smoked salmon, but it's actually a long-established partnership.
Puddings include good ices and a nice variation on bread and butter
pudding – Moriarty's barm brack and butter pudding with rum – or
there are Irish farmhouse cheeses to finish. Interesting and well-
priced wine list. Dinner only Tuesday-Saturday, 5.30-10; à la carte.

Closed Sunday & Monday and 1 November-16 March.

MasterCard, Visa.

Directions: Town centre.

KENMARE

Park Hotel Kenmare

Kenmare Co Kerry

Tel: 064 41200 Fax: 064 41402 email: phkenmare@iol.ie

This beautifully located Victorian railway hotel has earned international acclaim for exceptional standards of service, comfort and cuisine since 1985, when Francis Brennan became proprietor. Despite the constant quest for perfection, a warm welcome and the ever-burning fire in the hall ensure a relaxed atmosphere in antique-furnished public rooms that open onto an appealing verandah overlooking river and gardens. Luxurious suites and bedrooms are spacious, with all the comforts expected of top hotels. Equally, the elegant dining room provides a fitting setting for fine dinners: a stylishly restrained classicism and respect for local produce has characterised this distinguished kitchen under several famous head chefs. A short à la carte lounge menu is available, 11am-6pm. Superb attention to detail, in both the accommodation and restaurant, and caring service from an exceptional staff make a visit here truly memorable. Children welcome (to 8 pm in restaurant). Pets permitted in some areas; kennels available. 49 Rooms (12 no-smoking, 1 wheelchair friendly). Restaurant: 7-9 daily, dinner from £32. No smoking area. Toilets wheelchair accessible.

B&B £161 pps, single £168.

Hotel closed 2 January-13 April & 5 November-23 December.

Amex, Diners, MasterCard, Visa.

Directions: At the top of the town.

KENMARE   RESTAURANT/BAR

The Purple Heather

Henry Street Kenmare Co Kerry
Tel: 064 41016

In the O'Connell family since 1964, The Purple Heather has been run
by Grainne O'Connell since 1975 and was among the first to establish
a reputation for good food in Kenmare. In recent years it has become
the daytime sister restaurant to Packie's, where Grainne's sister
Maura is the proprietor-chef and, while the styles of the two
establishments may be superficially different, their dedication to
using the best local ingredients in sound, unpretentious cooking is a
shared commitment. The Purple Heather is a traditional darkwood
and burgundy bar that gradually develops into an informal
restaurant at the rear - a typically hospitable Kerry style that can be
found in many of the best establishments around the county. What
they aim for – and achieve, with commendable consistency – is good
home-cooked food: soups and home-baked breads, various salads of
organic greens and balsamic dressings, pâtés – including a delicious
smoked salmon pâté – a range of omelettes and Irish farmhouse
cheeses. Best of all, perhaps, is the fact that The Purple Heather is
open all year. Bar open 10.45am-7pm; food served 12-5 Monday-
Saturday

Closed Sunday, Christmas week & bank holidays.

No credit cards

Directions: Town centre.

KENMARE   COUNTRY HOUSE

Sallyport House

Kenmare Co Kerry
Tel: 064 42066 Fax: 064 42067

In a quiet and convenient location overlooking the harbour, with a
fine garden and mountain views at the rear, the Arthur family's
recently modernised house on the edge of Kenmare is spacious and
immaculately maintained throughout. The large entrance hall
exudes warmth, with its welcoming fire and richly-coloured rugs
and sets the tone for the high standard of accommodation offered.
Bedrooms are thoughtfully and very comfortably furnished with a
mixture of antique and good quality reproduction furniture - all
have orthopaedic beds, television (with video channel), direct
phones and (unusual enough to merit mention) well-positioned
lights and mirrors. Practical, fully-tiled bathrooms have powerful
over-bath showers and built in hair dryers and, under Janie Arthur's
eagle eye, housekeeping is outstanding. Delicious breakfasts are
served in a sunny dining room overlooking the garden. Ample
parking. Not suitable for children under 12. No dogs. 5 rooms (all
no-smoking).

B&B £45.50, single £70.

Closed November-Easter.

No credit cards.

Directions: South of town on N71, between town and bridge.

KENMARE   HOTEL/RESTAURANT

Sheen Falls Lodge

Kenmare Co Kerry
Tel: 064 41600 Fax: 064 41386
email: infor@sheenfallslodge.ie

Welcoming fires always burn in the foyer and the spacious, elegantly furnished reception rooms in this stunning hotel, including a lounge overlooking the waterfall. Luxurious rooms all have superb amenities, marbled bathrooms and views of the cascading river or Kenmare Bay. Facilities include a fine library, an equestrian centre and a Health Spa. **La Cascade Restaurant** - tiered to take full advantage of the waterfalls which are floodlit at night - features excellent modern Irish cooking on sensibly limited dinner menus characterised by vibrant flavours and perfect execution. The wine cellar is open for guests to choose their own bottle from nearly 500 wines and port can also be served in the cellar after dinner. But, like the nearby Park Hotel, it is the staff, under the guidance of the exceptionally warm and hospitable General Manager, Adriaan Bartels, who make this luxurious and stylish international hotel the home from home that it quickly becomes for each new guest. 61 rooms (10 no-smoking, 1 wheelchair friendly). Restaurant open 7.15-9.30. Dinner from £29.50.

Room rate £285 (1 or 2 guests).

Hotel closed 2 January-2 February, 2 -23 December.

Access, Amex, Visa, Diners.

Directions: Take N71 to Glengarriff, then first left after suspension bridge.

Shelburne Lodge

Killowen Cork Road Kenmare Co Kerry
Tel: 064 41013 Fax: 064 42135

A fine stone house on the edge of the town, Shelburne Lodge is the oldest house in Kenmare and is set back from the road in its own grounds and lovely gardens. It also has all the style, attention to detail and natural hospitality that would be expected from Tom and Maura Foley, proprietors of the dashing Kenmare restaurant, Packies. Spacious day rooms include an elegant, comfortable drawing room and a large, well-appointed dining room where excellent breakfasts are served. Accommodation, in seven rooms individually decorated to a high standard, is extremely comfortable and everything (especially beds and bedding) is of the highest quality; individual decoration extends to the excellent bathrooms – all with full bath except the more informal conversion at the back of the house, which is especially suitable for families and has neat shower rooms. No evening meals are served, but residents are directed to Packies.

Garden, tennis. Own parking. No pets. 9 rooms (2 shower-only).

B&B £45 pps, single £60

Closed 1 December- 27 February.

MasterCard, Visa.

Directions: on the Cork road R569, 500 yards from town centre, opposite the golf course.

Killarney

The fascination of Killarney is in its contrasts. The town is set amidst the most stunningly beautiful scenery - not just in Ireland, but in the entire world. The combination of a gentle climate with purple mountains, green hills, dark woods, tumbling rivers and silver lakes never fails to amaze and delight. Thus from the earliest stages of Killarney's development, the word "sublime" was the adjective most readily and accurately applied to the landscapes about it.

But amongst all this unspoilt natural magnificence, development is what Killarney is all about, and always has been. Only by accepting this can we begin to understand this bustling tourist town, where some of the crowded streets are so narrow that you're sometimes hard put to see the mountains at all.

If the story of global tourism development is ever written, Killarney will deserve a chapter to itself. Incredible as it may seem, it was as long ago as 1721 that the Catholic Earls of Kenmare set about creating a tourist centre in Killarney. The fourth Viscount Kenmare initiated a plan which resulted in New Street, Main Street and High Street - narrow thoroughfares by today's standards - being created around the site of an ancient church. Thus the shape of the central area of the modern town was literally set in stone.

Soon, in a time of increasing international prosperity, Killarney was right there with other famous European beauty spots and cultural centres as a "must see" destination on the Grand Tour - from which,

of course, we inherited our everyday word for visiting holiday-makers, or "tourists". Once, the traditional Kerry response to visitors praising their rugged landscape had been: "You can't eat scenery". But the Kenmare family - the Brownes - showed that, indirectly, you could. Their projects prospered, with the building of roads, hotels and inns, and the provision of boating amenities on the lakes both for fishing and sight-seeing - and, in 1861, Queen Victoria herself visited Killarney, putting the royal seal of approval on a destination that still has a hint of Victorian atmosphere today.

Today, Killarney is a year-round all-weather holiday town, re-inventing itself again as an up-market destination for the discerning traveller of the 21st century. The scenery and the "Kerry experience" are still there to be enjoyed in their timeless way and there's a wealth of activities and cultural experiences to enjoy, including golf, fishing, horseriding, walking and cycling for the energetic and gardens, museums, heritage centres, artists, craftworkers, traditional music, song and dance for relaxation. In Killarney itself, a long list of attractions include both Ireland's largest National Park, and Ireland's leading National Events Centre at the Gleneagle Hotel, which hosts international top acts and the hit Irish dance musical "To Dance on the Moon" which runs from May to September.

Underlying it all is the traditional Kerry instinct for hospitality. In Killarney, they make you feel welcome. They've been doing it for at

Photo - Traditional Farm at Muckross House

least three hundred years, and they have a real talent for it. Not suprisingly, many of Ireland's finest hoteliers are in Killarney; hospitality is in their blood and having had generations of experience they're at the forefront of the drive towards highlighting the best of accommodation of all types, and ensuring that dining experience for their guests includes gourmet restaurants at the highest level as well as good, informal choices.

Set amongst some of the most romantic scenery in Europe and with such outstanding hospitality on offer, perhaps the Killarney area especailly lives up to the promise "Kerry is for Lovers..."

KILLARNEY, AT AGHADOE   HOTEL/RESTAURANT

Aghadoe Heights Hotel

Aghadoe Killarney Co Kerry
Tel: 064 31766 Fax: 064 31345

This landmark 1960s hotel commands stunning views of Killarney's lakes and mountains, overlooks two 18-hole championship golf courses and has achieved a well-earned reputation for all-round excellence. After a change of ownership in 1997, major refurbishment was undertaken for the millennium and, while the architectural style is controversial, some aspects of the interior are impressive; new rooms, which include a presidential suite and 14 junior suites, have been equipped and furnished to high standards in a contemporary style, with private balconies. The whole hotel is spacious and luxuriously furnished and decorated, with lots of marble, antiques and good paintings. Panoramic views and Robin Suter's fine cuisine make a great combination at the first-floor restaurant, **Fredrick's**, now extended. Conference/banqueting and leisure facilities have also been increased and upgraded. Parking. Leisure centre, swimming pool, garden, tennis. Children welcome (Under 3s free in parents' room, cot available without charge). No pets. Restaurant 6.30-9.30 daily & Sunday 12.30-2; gourmet dinner £37.50. Rooms, 75 (all no-smoking, 1 for disabled).

B&B £110 pps, single £160.

Open all year.

Amex, Diners, MasterCard, Visa.

Directions: Just west of Killarney, well-signposted off the N22 road (both directions: Tralee and Cork)

KILLARNEY HOTEL

Arbutus Hotel

College Street Killarney
Tel: 064 31037 Fax: 064 34033
email:arbutushotel@eircom.ie

Named after a tree that grows prolifically in this part of the country (also known as the Strawberry Tree) this old hotel has been in the Buckley family since 1926 and has charm and personality that most newer ones lack. Since Sean Buckley took on the mantle in 1986, some major refurbishment has taken place - notably in 1997, when major work was done to 20 bedrooms, the foyer, restaurant and the lift. Sean aims to retain the old-world atmosphere of the hotel while providing the practical conveniences demanded by today's discerning traveller - and he is now gradually replacing the antiques which were discarded when the previous generation modernised the hotel some twenty years ago! Refurbished rooms, which are individually furnished and decorated, have direct-dial phones, multi-channel television with in-house video and tea/coffee making facilities. The oak-panelled hotel bar has a turf fire and real character - live traditional music is a regular feature and they take pride in serving a good pint. Children welcome (under 3s free in parents' room; cot available without charge). 35 rooms (3 shower only).

B&B £65 pps, single £85

Closed December & January.

Amex, Diners, MasterCard, Visa.

Directions: Killarney town centre.

KILLARNEY   GUESTHOUSE

Ashville Guesthouse

Rock Road Killarney Co Kerry
Tel: 064 36405 Fax: 064 36778
email ashvillelouse@eircom.net

Alma and Declan Walsh run a hands-on operation at their welcoming guesthouse, conveniently located just 2 minutes' walk from the town centre. Their twelve generously-sized en-suite bedrooms are furnished to a high standard with orthopaedic beds, direct dial phones, multi-channel television, tea/coffee-making facilities and hair dryer - and individually controlled heating. There's also a spacious sitting room with an open fire and an à la carte breakfast is served in a comfortable dining room furnished in country style. Numerous activities available in the area can be organised for guests, including outdoor pursuits like golf, fishing, cycling, horse riding and walking - and gentler outings such as a motor cruiser tour of the lakes and jaunting car rides for the less energetic. Own parking.

B&B £20-£28

Amex, MasterCard, Visa

Closed 18-30 December

Directions: On the main Tralee Road, N22.

KILLARNEY, AT BEAUFORT   BAR/RESTAURANT

Beaufort Bar & Restaurant

Beaufort Killarney Co Kerry
Tel: 064 44032 Fax: 064 44390

Padraig O'Sullivan's immaculate establishment is in the fourth generation of family ownership and, under his caring stewardship, recent major renovations have seen the old tree at the front left safely in place which, together with features like the stonework and an open fire in the bar for winter, have helped retain genuine character. The upstairs restaurant, which can be reached through the bar or by a separate entrance from the carpark, offers quite extensive à la carte dinner menus with a generous, traditional tone (seafood cocktail, chilled galia melon with a raspberry sorbet, chicken liver paté; roast Kerry lamb or duckling, sole meunière) and local ingredients such as Aghadoe black pudding receive special mention; finish with classic desserts or farmhouse cheeses. Pricing is fairly moderate and Sunday lunch especially good value. A private dining room for up to 40 is to be added this year. Own parking. Children welcome.

D Tue-Sat, 6.30-9.30, à la carte; L Sun only, 12.30-2.30

Closed 2 weeks in November & February; Sunday dinner, all Monday.

MasterCard, Visa.

Directions: Off N72 Killarney-Killorglin; turn left at Beaufort bridge - first stone building on the left.

KILLARNEY

RESTAURANT/CRAFT SHOP

Bricín

26 High Street Killarney Co Kerry
Tel: 064 34902 Fax: 064 39030

Paddy & Johnny McGuire's delightful country-style restaurant is on the first floor over an excellent craft shop which stocks an outstanding range of Irish pottery. Bricín has been restoring weary shoppers since 1990 and its large area is broken up into "rooms", which creates a surprisingly intimate atmosphere. The country mood suits head chef Maighread Forde's wholesome cooking: soups, salads and sandwiches are available all day and the lunch menu offers great value and good cooking in dishes like chicken pancakes with salad or chips, baked salmon in a white wine sauce with vegetables and potatoes and a vegetarian dish such as leek & lentil bake. Dinner menus move up a few gears, in starters like mussels in white wine sauce and main courses including rack of Kerry lamb, chargrilled fillet beef and the house specialty, Boxty, which comes with a variety of fillings and a mixed salad. Wine licence. No smoking area; air conditioning. Children welcome. Open Mon-Sat, 10-4.30; L 12.30-4.30; D 6-9.30 (early menu 6-7).

Closed Sunday, bank holidays; evenings November-March.

Amex, Diners, MasterCard, Visa.

Directions: Central Killarney; continuation of Main Street.

The Cooperage Restaurant

Old Market Lane Killarney Co Kerry
Tel: 064 37716 Fax: 064 37716 email chezmart@iol.ie

A friendly welcome and efficient service from the outset set the tone at Mo Stafford and head chef Martin McCormack's striking contemporary restaurant. Menus presented in a brand new reception area suggest a pleasing element of simplicity, recognition of seasonality and provenance of ingredients, as well as eye appeal; there's a shortish lunch menu, plus blackboard specials, with more choice in the evening. Stylish decor and moody background jazz are a reminder that The Cooperage was recently awarded the title of Rathborne Candles Atmospheric Restaurant of the Year. And the food lives up to the surroundings. Excellent soup - Mediterranean, perhaps - is a winner and unusual starters, like warm game baked loaf with plum chutney & tossed salad leaves, just beg to be tried. Main courses also include game in season and a selection of pasta and seafood dishes, such as baked seafood au gratin, with perfectly cooked vegetables. Finish with a delicious hazelnut meringue perhaps...A lively atmosphere and imaginative, well prepared food at reasonable prices ensure a loyal following here. No-smoking area; air conditioning.

L 12.30-3, D 6-10 Monday-Saturday. A la Carte. Toilets wheelchair accessible. Parking nearby.

Closed Sunday & evenings November-March. Open for lunch all year.

MasterCard, Visa.

Directions: Under the arch at Market Cross, Killarney main street.

KILLARNEY   RESTAURANT

Courtney's Restaurant

24 Plunkett Street Killarney Co Kerry
Tel/Fax: 064 32689

Anyone re-visiting what was once the "The Strawberry Tree" after a long absence will be pleased to find that, despite the new name, there are few obvious changes at this characterful restaurant under new ownership - and head chef Eileen O'Brien remains the power in the kitchen. As before, she upholds a policy of commitment to wild, organic and free-range produce as far as possible, with the eventual aim of being 100% organic - and the high standard of cooking remains, of course, the same. The provenenace of some ingredients is given - 'old fashioned farmed duck', for example, comes from Dennis Barry's farm - and others are specified as free-range or wild. Menus are as exciting as ever, with starters like Darjeeling tea cured salmon and warm salad of Guinness-battered black pudding over a mixed salad with warm apple dressing and main courses are strong on game (in summer this might be rabbit, pigeon and venison) and organic Kerry beef. Delicious desserts - or the cheeseboard - are always worth saving room for. Not suitable for children under 12. Dinner Monday-Saturday, 6.30-10. Limited bar food 12.30-8.

Closed on Sunday.

Mastercard, Visa.

Directions: Centrally located in Plunkett Street, in the heart of Killarney.

KILLARNEY   HOTEL/RESTAURANT

Dromhall Hotel & Kayne's Bistro

Muckross Road Killarney Co Kerry
Tel: 064 31431 Fax: 064 34242

An impressive reception area, well-appointed public areas and unsually spacious bedrooms with well-designed bathrooms, all create a good impression in the completely re-built Dromhall Hotel which opened in summer 2000. The stylish ground floor Kayne's Bar & Bistro, which has its own entrance, is spacious and pleasantly furnished, with welcome attention to comfort as well as eye-appeal. It's an agreeable place to drop into at any time of day, whether for a quick cup of coffee or a bite from a lively menu including colourful dishes like bruschetta with sundried tomato, mozzarella, basil & olive oil, char-grilled chicken strips with tossed leaves & spices sausage and an imaginative range of sandwiches. Restaurant menus offer a wider choice of about twelve appealing contemporary dishes on each course, everything is cooked to order and vegetarian dishes are considerably highlighted.

A brand new leisure centre situated between the Dromhall and its sister hotel Randles, is for their common use. Ample parking. Lift. 70 rooms (3 for disabled). Bar meals 12.30-6.30 daily;

Restaurant 6.30-10 daily.

B&B £50 pps, single £70.

Closed Christmas week.

Diners, MasterCard, Visa.

Directions: On right entering Killarney by Muckross Road, beside Randles Hotel.

KILLARNEY   GUESTHOUSE

Earls Court House

Woodlawn Junction Muckross Road Killarney Co Kerry
Tel: 064 34009 Fax: 064 34366 email: earls@eircom.net

Roy and Emer Moynihan's purpose-built guesthouse is quite near the town centre and provides hotel-standard accommodation and caring owner-management at a fairly moderate price. The Earls Court House has also gained a reputation for its collection of antiques and the generous scale of the house allows them to be displayed to advantage: comfortable seating groups are arranged around a large foyer with an open fire, where afternoon tea and drinks are served. Spacious, well-planned bedrooms, which are individually decorated to provide modern comforts with old-fashioned ambience, all have queen size orthopaedic beds, good bathrooms with tubs and power showers, satellite TV and direct dial phone with modem. Tea/coffee making facilities are available on request. Breakfast is served in a pleasant dining; limited room service is also available, also drying and ironing facility for laundry. Children welcome (under 2s free, cot available without charge). No pets. Private parking. 11 rooms (some no smoking).

B&B £48 pps, single £68.

Closed 7 November-15 February.

MasterCard, Visa.

Directions: Off N71 Killarney-Kenmare: first left after the filling station on the left; 3rd entrance on left.

KILLARNEY   GUESTHOUSE/RESTAURANT

Foley's Townhouse & Restaurant

23 High Street Killarney Co Kerry
Tel: 064 31217 Fax: 064 34683

A Killarney landmark for many years, Foley's was originally a 19th century coaching inn and has seen many generations of travellers cross the threshold. The current owners, Denis and Carol Hartnett, have been here since 1967 and their 28 rooms are individually decorated and furnished to a high standard with television, phone and double glazing - and particularly attractive bathrooms with many touches usually associated with the better hotels. Residents have their own entrance, a residents' lounge and separate dining room. Next door, a cosy front bar is furnished to encourage lingering by the open fire while the main restaurant it opens onto is much more businesslike, with rows of white-clothed tables indicating that a high level of turnover should be expected in high season. Seafood and steaks are the specialities of the house; fairly traditional menus based on local produce are prepared under Carol Hartnett's personal supervision. Private parking.

B&B £45.50

Accommodation closed 1 November-4 April

Amex MasterCard, Visa

Directions: Town centre

KILLARNEY   GUESTHOUSE

Fuchsia House

Muckross Road Killarney Co Kerry
Tel: 064 33743 Fax: 064 36588

On arrival at this purpose-built guesthouse - just a short walk from the town centre and set well back from the road in a lovely front garden - you'll be served tea and home-made cake in the drawing room, a prelude to an outstanding breakfast the next morning. The spacious bedrooms, which include some suites added this year, are all luxuriously furnished with quality fabrics and bedding (the beds are especially firm and comfortable) and have facilities more usually associated with expensive hotels, including remote-control satellite TV and direct-dial telephone, a professional hairdryer and power shower in the well-equipped bathrooms. Hosts Tom and Mary Treacy are part of a family of well-known and dedicated Killarney hoteliers (Killarney Lodge, Killarney Park and Ross Hotels), ensuring the house is immaculately run and maintained. A large conservatory for guests' use overlooks the attractively laid out back garden. Wheelchair accessible. Children welcome (under 10s free in parents room; cots available; childrens' playground.) No Pets.

10 rooms (all en-suite & no smoking). Ample car parking.

B&B £42pps, single £62.

Closed 15 November-1 March. Diners, MasterCard, Visa.

Directions: On the N71 to Kenmare, on the right hand side.

KILLARNEY   RESTAURANT

Gaby's Seafood Restaurant

27 High Street Killarney Co Kerry
Tel: 064 32519 Fax: 064 32747

Gaby's is one of Ireland's longest established seafood restaurants, famous throughout the country for chef-proprietor Gert Maes' well-designed seasonal à la carte menus in classic French style – and in three languages. There's a cosy little bar beside an open fire just inside the door and several steps up to the main dining area, which is cleverly broken up into sections and has a pleasantly informal atmosphere. Absolute freshness is the priority – a note on the menu reminds that availability depends on daily landings – but there's always plenty else to choose from, with steaks and local lamb as back-up. Specialities include wild Atlantic salmon, with chive & lemon cream and red onion marmalade, Atlantic prawns on a bed of tagliatelle in a light garlic sauce and lobster "Gaby": fresh lobster, cognac, wine, cream and spices - cooked to a secret recipe. Lovely desserts include "my mother's recipe" - an old-fashioned apple & raspberry crumble - or you can finish with an Irish cheese selection.

Toilets wheelchair accessible. Dinner Monday-Sat 6-10pm; à la carte.

Closed Sunday, 20 December-3 January & mid February-mid March.

Amex, Diners, MasterCard, Visa.

Directions: Town centre, on the main street.

KILLARNEY, AT BEAUFORT   HOTEL

Hotel Dunloe Castle

Beaufort Killarney Co Kerry
Tel: 064 44111 Fax: 064 44583

Loved by many for wonderful gardens, which are home to an award-winning collection of subtropical trees and shrubs from all over the world, this luxurious sister hotel to the Hotel Europe (Fossa) and Ard-na-Sidhe (Caragh Lake), has many features in common with the larger Europe: the style of the building is similar, the same priorities apply – generous space is allowed for all areas throughout, the quality of furnishing is exceptionally high and both maintenance and housekeeping are superb. Using local produce like Kerry lamb and wild salmon is a point of pride in the restaurant, which has a lovely view out over the hotel's gardens and grazing horses in the paddocks to the Gap of Dunloe. The original castle is still part of the development, but the hotel is mainly modern and, like the Europe, the atmosphere is distinctly continental. Major developments are taking place as we go to press, so the 2001 season should see a much changed Hotel Dunloe Castle. Leisure centre, swimming pool. Children welcome playroom, playground). Pets permitted. Lift. 110 rooms (including 1 suite).

B&B £132 (room rate for two with breakfast, single £114).

Closed 1 October-mid April.

Amex, Diners, MasterCard, Visa.

Directions: off main Ring of Kerry road.

KILLARNEY, AT FOSSA HOTEL

Hotel Europe

Fossa Killarney Co Kerry
Tel: 064 31900 Fax: 064 32118
email: sales@kih.liebherr.com

Luxurious, generous in scale and exceptionally well-built, this immaculately maintained 1960s hotel still outshines many a new top level establishment. Public areas are very large and impressive, furnished to the highest standards and make full use of the hotel's wonderful location. Leisure facilities include a 25-metre swimming pool and seaweed bath, originally dating back to the time of the hotel's construction – a credit to the vision and wisdom of the developers. Bedrooms follow a similar pattern, with lots of space, best quality furnishings, beautiful views - and balconies on lakeside rooms. The hotel's continental connections show clearly in the style throughout but especially, perhaps, when it comes to food - breakfast, for example, is a hot and cold buffet; however, head chef Willie Steinbeck and his team take pride is sourcing the best of Irish produce, such as Kerry lamb and local seafood for the hotel's well-named **Panorama Restaurant**, which overlooks the lakes.Leisure centre, swimming pool. Equestrian, fishing, tennis, cycling, snooker. Children welcome (playroom, playground). Pets permitted. Lift. 204 rooms (8 suites, 42 junior suites)

B&B £124 for two; single £114

Closed mid-November - mid-March.

Amex, Diners, MasterCard, Visa.

Directions: On main Ring of Kerry road.

KILLARNEY

Kathleen's Country House

Madam's Height Tralee Road Killarney Co Kerry
Tel: 064 32810 Fax: 064 32340 email: info@kathleens.net

Setting standards in hospitality since 1980 (when it was among the first to offer hotel standards at guesthouse prices), Kathleen O'Regan Sheppard's family-run business continues to offer guests outstanding hospitality, comfort and good value in this large house set quietly in landscaped gardens just a mile from the town centre. The individually decorated rooms are all non-smoking and furnished to a high standard, with orthopaedic beds, phone, TV, tea/coffee-making facilities and fully tiled bathrooms have both bath and shower. Constant maintenance and refurbishment ensures that everything is immaculate, including several sitting rooms and comfortable seating areas that provide plenty of room for groups of varying sizes to relax. Caring service and original art all through the house add greatly to the feeling of being in a special place - and breakfasts that are themselves a work of art are served in a pleasant dining room overlooking the garden.

Parking. Wheelchair accessible. Not suitable for very young children (over 7s welcome). Rooms 17 (all no smoking, 2 for wheelchair users).

B&B £45 pps, single £80.

Closed 7 November-7 March.

Amex, MasterCard, Visa.

Directions: 1 mile north of Killarney town, off Tralee road (N 22).

Killarney Great Southern Hotel

Killarney Co Kerry

Tel: 064 31262 Fax: 064 31642 email: res@killarney.gsh.ie

An impressive pillared entrance and ivy-clad facade convey a sense of occasion at this classic Victorian railway hotel, which is set in 36 acres of landscaped gardens. Recent refurbishments have been completed with respect for the hotel's age and history: the spacious foyer, especially, has retained its grandeur and other public areas - including a homely residents' drawing room and a fine bar - are elegant, high-ceilinged rooms with a soothing atmosphere. Similarly, ongoing renovation of bedrooms is improving standards of comfort dramatically.

Peppers at the Southern, a lovely new bistro-style restaurant which opened in the summer of 2000, makes a brilliant alternative the main hotel dining room. Situated quietly in a corner position behind the bar and overlooking the gardens, it is dashingly decorated in the modern idiom, with high-back chairs, an elegant black, brown and beige/gold colour scheme and (in common with other areas of the hotel) fine paintings. The ambience, professional service and head chef Fintan Ryan's imaginative menus and sound cooking have made it an immediate success and - unusually for an hotel restaurant - it is now established as one of Killarney's leading eating places.

Swimming pool. Wheelchair accessible. Children welcome. Pets permitted by arrangement. 181 rooms (1 for wheelchair users).

B&B £92 pps, single £114; 12.5% s.c.

Peppers: 6.30-9.30 Monday-Saturday, closed Sunday; à la carte

Amex, Diners, MasterCard, Visa. Open all year

Directions: Town centre, beside the railway station.

KILLARNEY   GUESTHOUSE

Killarney Lodge

Countess Road Killarney Co Kerry
Tel: 064 36499 Fax: 064 31070 email: kylodge@iol.ie

Catherine Treacy's fine purpose-built guesthouse is set in private walled gardens just a two minute walk from the town centre. It has large en-suite air-conditioned bedrooms with all the amenities expected of an hotel room and spacious public rooms to relax in, including guest sitting rooms with open fires and a well-appointed dining room where an extensive breakfast menu is served. Catherine is a member of the well-known Killarney hotelier family, the Treacys, (Killarney Park Hotel, The Ross Hotel etc) and her professionalism has earned Killarney Lodge a reputation for service, hospitality and a relaxed atmosphere. Garden. Parking. Children welcome. Wheelchair accessible. No pets.16 rooms (all no smoking; 2 junior suites, 14 executive; 1 shower only, suitable for wheelchair users).

B&B £42 pps, single £70.

Closed 6 November-31 January.

Amex, Diners, MasterCard, Visa.

Directions: Two minutes walk from Town centre off Muckross road.

KILLARNEY   HOTEL/RESTAURANT

Killarney Park Hotel

Kenmare Place Killarney Co Kerry
Tel: 064 35555 Fax: 064 35266 email: info@killarneypark.ie

Although only a decade old, the Treacy family's charming hotel has a luxurious Victorian country house atmosphere - partly due to the elegant design of the building, its timeless decor and open fires, but also the friendliness of the staff and that unmistakable feeling of caring hands-on management and attention to detail.

A sweeping staircase leads to suites and bedrooms, all individually furnished to a very high standard; constant refurbishment has ensured that everything is always fresh and bright - and the same applies to the much older sister property nearby, the Ross Hotel, which is equally delightful.

Restaurant: In this opulent room a pianist plays throughout dinner and locally sourced food is presented with pride and style: standards of food and service have always far surpassed that normally expected of a hotel dining room.

Toilets wheelchair accessible. Air conditioning. Leisure centre. Snooker. Garden. No Pets. Children welcome. Lift. 76 rooms & suites (30 no-smoking, 1 suitable for wheelchair users).

B&B £240 (room rate, 2 guests)

Dinner 7-9.30 daily (Set menu £33; also à la carte); Lunch Sunday only, £18.

Hotel closed 23-26 December.

Amex, Diners, MasterCard, Visa

Directions: Town centre, next to Killarney Great Southern Hotel.

KILLARNEY   HOTEL

Killarney Royal

College Street Killarney Co Kerry
Tel: 064 31853 Fax: 064 34001 email royalhot@iol.ie

Joe and Margaret Scallys' charming town centre hotel is the older sister of their larger Hayfield Manor Hotel in Cork city and has recently completed a major refurbishment programme. The results, in an elegant period style that is totally appropriate to the age and design of the building, are very impressive: no expense has been spared to ensure the highest quality of materials and workmanship, air conditioning has been installed throughout the hotel and rooms have been individually designed, all with marble bathrooms and sitting areas. But it is perhaps the level of service provided that attracts most praise - after three generations the Scallys see excellence as the main ingredient for success and this is seen in their staff's genuine desire to please Wheelchair accessible. Arrangement with nearby carpark. Children welcome. No pets 24 hour room service. 29 rooms (including 5 suites & 5 no-smoking rooms).

B&B £105 pps, ss £45.

Closed 22-28 December.

Amex, Diners, MasterCard, Visa.

Directions: Town centre of Killarney ; College Street, off the N22.

KILLARNEY, AT AGHADOE   HOTEL/RESTAURANT

Killeen House Hotel

Aghadoe Killarney Co Kerry
Tel: 064 31711 Fax: 064 31811
email: charming@indigo.ie

Michael and Geraldine Rosney's "charming little hotel" is an early nineteenth century rectory just 10 minutes drive from Killarney town centre and 5 minutes from Killeen and Mahoney's Point golf courses. You don't have to be a golfer to stay here but it must help, especially in the pubby little bar, which is run as an "honour" bar with guest's golf balls accepted as tender. The bonhomie, which includes addressing guests by first names from the start, is clearly relished by most visitors and nothing is too much trouble to ensure that guests can reach their golfing appointments on distant courses, at whatever time. Rooms vary in size but all have full bathrooms (one with jacuzzi) and are freshly-decorated, with phone and satellite TV. There's a traditional drawing room with an open fire for guests and the dining room is open to non-residents. Children welcome. Pets permitted by arrangement. 23 rooms. Dinner 7-10 daily; set menu £29.50; sc 10%.

B&B £47.50 pps, single £67.50.

Closed 1 Nov - 1 April.

Amex, Diners, MasterCard, Visa.

Directions: 4 miles from Killarney - just off Dingle road.

KILLARNEY HOTEL

Lake Hotel

Muckross Road Killarney Co Kerry
Tel: 064 31035 Fax: 064 31902
email: lakehotel@eircom.net

Set well back from the road right on the lake shore, with the ruins
of McCarthy Mor Castle within the grounds, the Lake Hotel is in a
unique shoreside position and has a fascinating history. It was built
in 1820, in the heyday of Victorian tourism, and visited by Queen
Victoria when she came to Ireland in 1861 - the hotel still has the
original horse-drawn carriage in which she travelled. Public areas
include a spacious lounge with a big log fire, television room and
the lively Devils Punchbowl Bar, with traditional music in summer.
All bedrooms are comfortably furnished and have the usual modern
amenities; recently added rooms include suites with four-poster
beds, spa bath and private balconies overlooking the lakes - and
some unusual new themed suites are to be available for 2001. Own
fishing. Tennis. Children welcome (under 3s free in parents room;
cots available, playroom). Wheelchair accessible. No Pets. Lift.
Rooms 70 (2 rooms for disabled; 2 shower only).

B&B about £40 pps, single £57

Closed 4 December-12 February.

Amex, Diners, MasterCard, Visa.

Directions: 1 mile from Killarney town on the road to Kenmare.

KILLARNEY   HOTEL

Randles Court Clarion Hotel

Muckross Road Killarney Co Kerry
Tel: 064 35333 Fax: 064 35206 email: randles@iol.ie

Originally built in 1906 as a private residence, this attractive house underwent extensive refurbishment before opening as an hotel in 1992 under the caring owner-management of the Randles family. Although it has grown a little since then, period features including fireplaces and stained glass windows, have been retained and it still has the domesticity and warmth of a family home. Bedrooms are spacious and furnished to a high standard, with direct dial telephones, satellite television, radio, hair dryers and well-appointed bathrooms. Comfortably furnished public rooms include a small bar, a large drawing room with log fire, tapestries and antiques and the dashing **Checkers Restaurant** which opens onto a sheltered patio and has a striking black and white theme, softened by a trompe l'oeil wall. Head chef Enda Currayne, who has been with the hotel since 1994, takes pride in sourcing the best local produce and presenting it in classics like prime medallion of beef flamed in cognac and finished with a peppercorn sauce. New leisure facilities are shared with the neighbouring sister establishment Dromhall Hotel. Own parking. No pets. 50 rooms (including 2 suites, 12 junior suites & 1 suitable for wheelchair users).

B&B £70 pps, Single £100

Closed Christmas week.

Amex, Diners, MasterCard, Visa.

Directions: On the right, heading into Killarney from Muckross.

KILLARNEY RESTAURANT

West End House

Lower New Street Killarney Co Kerry
Tel: 064 32271 Fax: 064 35979

The Fassbenders' unusual restaurant has a somewhat Tyrolean atmosphere and an interesting history, having once been (most appropriately) one of Ireland's oldest schools of housewifery. Today it ranks as one of the "old guard" in Killarney hospitality terms as it has been serving wholesome, hearty fare at lunch and dinner without fuss or ostentation for many years and has earned a great reputation for reliability. The surroundings are simple but comfortable - a fireplace set at a sensibly high level in the wall at the end of the bar casts warmth across the room, which can be very welcome on chilly evenings - and the cooking is comfortingly traditional in a strong house style untroubled by fashion. Local produce is used to advantage, typically in good home-made soups that come with freshly-baked bread, main courses such as rack of Kerry lamb.

Closed Monday.

Mastercard, Visa.

Directions: Opposite St Mary's Church.

Photo - Fishing on Caragh river, Killorglin

Killorglin

All Kerry's towns have individual character, and Killorglin is highly individual. It is the setting for Puck Fair, a happening so ancient it probably has its roots in pre-Christian times.

Officially, it's a horse fair. But as the hilly little town is the market centre for some of the best farmland in Kerry, there's all sorts of trading. And there's more to it than that. As the Fair approaches in mid-August, a wild mountain goat is captured in the nearby MacGillycuddy's Reeks.

On the first day of Puck Fair, he is hoisted to the top of a specially consructed tower in the middle of town, and for three days he is feted as King Puck, with horns garlanded as befits his elevated status.

In the streets below, Killorglin has all the fun of the fair, and then some. This ancient festival has a special appeal for country people and travelling folk from every part of Ireland. The rest of the time, Killorglin is a busy little country town with some attractive traditional shop fronts, and many fine old pubs. But always, there's a certain sense of mystery as you reflect on the ancient rites of Puck Fair.

KILLORGLIN RESTAURANT/BAR

Nick's Seafood Restaurant & Piano Bar

Lower Bridge Street Killorglin Co Kerry
Tel: 066 976 1219 / 976 1936 Fax: 066 976 1233

Nick and Anne Foley started up here in 1978 and, aside from providing excellent food, Nick's is has always been renowned for its music and great atmosphere. Nick Foley's cooking – classic French with an Irish accent– has earned a particular reputation for his way with local seafood, although there are always other choices, notably prime Kerry fillet steak and rack of Kerry lamb. Specialities include lobster from their own tank and lobster thermidor, moules marinière or provençale, shellfish mornay and peppered steak in brandy cream sauce are all typical of his classic style. Vegetarians aren't forgotten either – there's a choice of three dishes on the regular menu. Dessert choices are changed daily and there's a good cheeseboard. [*The Foleys have bought the Church of Ireland premises next door and plan to develop it, so there may soon be dramatic changes to the premises.]

Children welcome. No-smoking area; air conditioning. Extensive wine list.

Restaurant 6.30-10 (Wednesday-Sunday in winter, daily in summer). Dinner menu £28, also à la carte.

Closed all November; 24-25 December; Monday & Tuesday December-March.

Amex, Diners, MasterCard, Visa.

Directions: On the Ring of Kerry road 12 miles from Killarney.

Photo - Mairéad McGuinness, presenter of RTE's 'Ear to the Ground' farming programme, at the opening of the Listowel Quality Food Fair

Listowel

Elegantly situated above a sweeping bend in the River Feale, Listowel is the thriving market town and touring centre of northeast Kerry. It is famed equally for the remarkable literary output of its citizens, and the sport to be enjoyed at its popular race course, which makes full use of the large area of level ground within the curve of the meandering river.

Listowel Writers' Week, usually in late May, has become an internationally renowned gathering for wordsmiths, and the celebration of the town's many authors is only part of its activities. However, the fact that Listowel can include amongst its literary sons such luminaries as playwright George Fitzmaurice, novelist Maurice Walsh, who wrote The Quiet Man, historian Anthony Gaughan, poet and author Bryan MacMahon, and the famous playwright-publican John B Keane, is a matter for celebration at any time of the year and in many places.

But nevertheless it is something which brings a special enjoyment to visiting Listowel. As for the horse racing - dating from 1858, and inspiring a poetry of its own - the most popular meeting is in late September, when writers and horse enthusiasts alike can enjoy the fact that Listowel has fifty pubs.

LISTOWEL   RESTAURANT/BAR/ACCOMMODATION

Allo's Bar & Bistro

41 Church Street Listowel Co Kerry
Tel/Fax: 068 22880

Armel Whyte and Helen Mullane's café-bar was established in 1859
and is named after the previous owner, Alphonsus, known as "Allo".
Since they took over in 1995, major restoration work has been
sensitively completed using salvaged building materials - and items
like the flooring, which was once in the London Stock Exchange, are
a great talking point. The long, narrow bar is divided up in the
traditional way and their ever-growing collection of antiques,
informal dining arrangements, genuine friendliness and Armel's
lively cooking - traditional and new Irish cooking with some
international influences, all based on carefully sourced local
ingredients - add up to a place of character.

Accommodation: Extending into the house next door in 1999
allowed the addition of three beautiful guest bedrooms. Spacious
and stylishly furnished with antiques, they have four-poster beds
and luxurious Connemara marbled bathrooms (one with shower
only).

No smoking area. Toilets wheelchair accessible.

Food available 12-9 Monday-Saturday. A la carte; also Set Dinner £25.

B&B £45, single £60.

Establishment closed Sundays, 25 December & Good Friday.

Amex, MasterCard, Visa.

Directions: Approaching on N69, halfway down Church Street on the
right -look for the bay trees outside the door.

LISTOWEL   HOTEL

Listowel Arms Hotel

The Square Listowel Co Kerry
Tel: 068 21500 Fax: 068 22524

Set comfortably in a corner of the old town square, this much-loved old hotel is rich in history: political giants like Daniel O'Connell and Charles Stewart Parnell are among the many famous people who have stayed here and - appropriately as it is now the main venue for the annual Listowel Writers Week - the Victorian author William Thackeray recommended the hotel as far back as 1842. Since 1996 the hotel has been blessed with the energetic and discerning ownership of Kevin O'Callaghan, who has since overseen a major extension and overhaul of the whole premises The extension has provided a new restaurant, kitchen, banqueting area and new bedrooms, all overlooking the River Feale. Improvements previously made to the existing building have all been done with admirable sensitivity, so greater comfort has been gained without loss of character. Wheelchair accessible. Lift. Children welcome Pets permitted by arrangement. 37 rooms.

B&B from £35 pps. (Higher rates apply to race and festival weeks).

Closed 24-26 December.

Directions: In the corner of the old square in Listowel town centre.

Photo - Glanleam House and Gardens on Valentia Island, just across the bridge from Portmagee.

Portmagee

Portmagee is Kerry's most westerly fishing port, which makes it the furthest west in Ireland and Europe as well. It's a very sea-minded little place, with its colourful waterfront looking across a sheltered channel which provides convenient access to the open Atlantic.

And out in that open Atlantic, there soar those mighty rocks, the Skelligs. Atop the highest of them - Skellig Michael - there are the remarkably well-preserved remains of a miniature monastery. Here, more than a thousand years ago, the monks of old did more than merely survive - they prospered, and preserved civilised ways of thought as the rest of Europe sank into the Dark Ages.

The channel which gives Portmagee its natural harbour is the sound inside Valentia Island. The bridge across it at Portmagee was completed as recently as 1971, and on the island side, the Skelligs Experience Interpretive Centre gives a fascinating insight into those extraordinary islands.

And if weather conditions permit, skilled crews with fast modern boats can take you to sea to savour the Skelligs in all their glory, an awe-inpiring experience which will make the friendly hostelries of Portmagee seem even more welcoming on your safe return.

PORTMAGEE GUESTHOUSE/RESTAURANT/PUB

The Moorings

Portmagee Co Kerry
Tel: 066 947 7108 Fax: 066 947 7220
email: moorings@iol.ie

Gerard & Patricia Kennedy's fine guesthouse overlooks the picturesque fishing port at Portmagee and many bedrooms have a sea view. All are comfortably furnished in a warm contemporary style and have good amenities including direct-dial phones, television, tea/coffee making facilities and well-designed bathrooms with both bath and shower. Seafood stars in the à la carte restaurant and the style is fairly traditional - chowder, seafood selection, deep-fried brie for starters; main courses of seafood platter, poached salmon, steaks - and lobster, which is quite moderately priced. The Bridge Bar, next door, is also run by the family so this is more like an inn than a guesthouse and restaurant: the restaurant is only open in the evnings except for Sunday lunch, but you can get informal meals from noon everyday in the bar. Trips to Skellig Michael can be arranged and there's on-site entertainment later too, as the bar also becomes a lively venue for music, song and dance at night. Children welcome. No pets. 14 rooms.

B&B £30 pps, single £38.

Restaurant closed Monday, except July-August.

Establishment closed 1 November-1 March.

Mastercard, Visa.

Directions: Turn right 3 miles outside Caherciveen, on the Waterville road.

Photo - The Kerry Way, near Sneem

Sneem

Sneem is soporific, but in the pleasantest possible way. Its bright little houses, pubs and shops are painted in vivid colours which help to keep you awake as you enjoy this friendly stopover on the famous Ring of Kerry.

For although the Ring of Kerry includes some of the most spectacular mountain scenery in Ireland, Sneem itself is set in gentler territory on the sun-warmed south-facing coast along the north shore of the Kenmare River, among secret islands and hidden creeks.

It's a place with an astonishingly gentle climate, and all along the coast from Sneem up to Kenmare itself, you'll find pleasant pockets of civilisation where life can be taken at its own gentle pace.

And enjoyed for a long time, too. Midway between Sneem and Kenmare, the valley of the River Blackwater winds northwards and upwards towards the purple peaks of Mullaghanattin and Knocklomena. It's said that along this gentle little river, people live longer than anywhere else in Ireland. Nearby, another sweet place is Tahilla - not so much a village, more a state of mind. And that state of mind is at peace with the world.

Great Southern Hotel Parknasilla

Parknasilla Sneem Co Kerry
Tel: 064 45122 Fax: 064 45323
email: res@parknasilla.gsh.ie

Set in 300 acres of sub-tropical parkland, this classic Victorian hotel overlooking Kenmare Bay is blessed with one of the most beautiful locations in Ireland. In the spacious foyer, antiques and fresh flowers set a tone of quiet luxury which is enhanced by the hotel's collection of original art (currently being catalogued). Excellent amenities for both activity and relaxation include an outdoor swimming pool and Canadian hot tub - and an abundance of comfortable places (including a no-smoking drawing room) for a quiet read or afternoon tea. Public rooms include an impressive restaurant and a library, added in 1995 for the hotel's centenary. Bedrooms vary in size and outlook but all have en-suite bathrooms with bath and shower, direct-dial telephone, radio, TV with in-house movie channel, trouser press and hair dryer. Tea/coffee making facilities are also available. Leisure centre, swimming pool. Golf, tennis, snooker, fishing, equestrian, walking. Wheelchair accessible. Children welcome. No Pets. 84 rooms (including 1 suite, 8 junior-suites, 13 executive, 1 suitable for wheelchair users).

B&B £120 pps, single £122.

Open all year.

Amex, Diners, MasterCard, Visa.

Directions: 30 miles outside Killarney, past Kenmare en route to Sneem.

SNEEM GUESTHOUSE

Tahilla Cove Country House

Tahilla Sneem Co Kerry
Tel: 064 45204 Fax: 064 45104
email: tahillacove@eircom.net

In an idyllic setting on the Ring of Kerry shoreside, this family-run guesthouse is a low-key place, with an old country house in there somewhere (much added to) but an away-from-it-all atmosphere and caring hands-on management by the owners, James and Deirdre Waterhouse, make it really special. It feels like a small hotel – it has a proper bar, for example, which is used by locals as well as residents (bar food available noon-7pm). All the public rooms have views, including a large sitting room, with plenty of armchairs and sofas, which opens onto a terrace overlooking the garden and the cove with its little stone jetty: comfort and relaxation are the priorities. Rooms vary considerably but most have sea views, many have balconies and all have phone, television, hair-dryer and individually controlled heating. Non-residents are welcome for dinner when there is room. Wheelchair accessible. Children welcome. Pets permitted in some areass. 9 rooms (1 shower only).

B&B £43 pps, single £63

Closed mid-October-Easter.

Amex, Diners, MasterCard, Visa.

Directions: On the northern side of Kenmare Bay (route N70). Ring of Kerry 11 miles west of Kenmare and 5 miles east of Sneem.

Photo - Tralee Golf Club

Tralee

The business of Tralee is business. It is the County Town and the Kingdom's leading commercial centre, so much so that the buzz of the place will add spice to any visit, even if your main reason for going to Kerry is enjoyment of the deep peace to be found in the mountains and on the coast.

But as it happens, even with all its energetic bustle, Tralee can be an ideal holiday base. It has the convenience of the railhead furthest from Dublin, yet with regular train connections with both Dublin and Cork. And Kerry Airport at Farranfore is only eleven miles up the road.

Then too, when you look at what the neighbourhood has to offer, it soon becomes clear that Tralee is a worthwhile holiday destination in its own right. The main port on lovely Tralee Bay may now be out at Fenit, but properly speaking, Fenit is part of Tralee. It's at the west end of a balmy south-facing coast, with all amenities including the Seaworld exhibition and a marina which has raised Tralee Bay's attractions even further for visiting leisure sailors.

In Tralee itself, the Ship Canal is being re-opened, bringing an added sense of the sea right into the town centre. And if you follow the short canal on its progress towards the bay, you'll soon reach Blennerville, home to one of the largest working windmills in Ireland, a vividly white structure which dominates the view for miles around.

Mention Tralee anywhere in the world, and people will talk of the Rose of Tralee. Based on a moving song written in 1845, today's Rose of Tralee Festival, held annually in late August, is an extraordinary celebration of the Irish diaspora, and the way that any country in the world can provide a lovely girl of Irish ancestry enthusiastically willing to take part in this unique beauty and personality contest.

Tralee also provides much of interest and enjoyment for families on holiday. There is Aqua Dome, which is the largest weather-independent attraction of its type in Ireland, plus the Siamsa Tire Folk Theatre, and also Kerry the Kingdom exhibition in the Ashe Memorial Hall. As for sport, there's greyhound racing at the well-furnished Kingdom Stadium every Tuesday and Friday night, and on Saturdays in summer, there's also horse racing, and of course there's golf in abundance.

Access to Co. Kerry

By Air

Kerry airport is located at Farranfore, just 20 minutes from Tralee and 15 minutes from Killarney. For flight information telephone Kerry airport (066) 976 4644. See also Aer Arann schedule on page 14.

By Rail

Irish rail operate daily mainline rail services from Dublin, Cork and Roslare to Killarney, Farranfore and Tralee.

For information telephone

Tralee - talking timetable (066) 712 3566

Killarney   (064) 31067

Bus Eireann

Expressway coaches link Kerry with locations nationwide. Telephone:

Killarney   (064) 34777

Tralee   (066) 712 3566

Denny's
Finest
Ham

DENNY

Finest

COOKED HAM

This premium quality ham is cured using a traditional Denny recipe for that unique Denny taste.

4 SLICES

WEIGHT **120g** ℮

Keep Refrigerated below 4°C.
Eat within 48 hours of opening.

PRICE	USE BY

MADE TO DISAPPEAR

TRALEE   HOTEL

Abbey Gate Hotel

Tralee Co Kerry
Tel: 066 712 9888 Fax: 066 712 9821
email:abbeygate@iol.ie

Conveniently situated in a relatively quiet corner in the centre of
Tralee, this large modern hotel provides a wide range of amenities
for both business and leisure guests. A spacious marble-floored
foyer has an imposing marble fireplace and ample seating space,
making it an excellent meeting place both for residents and locals
going to the main Vineyard Restaurant, which serves dinner
Tuesday-Saturday and Sunday lunch, or the informal little Bistro
Marché, which is open every evening. There's also a traditional-style
pub, The Market Place, a where bar food is served all day; this big
bar can be a very lively venue, but it's broken down into smaller
areas and this, plus the use of natural materials and open
fireplaces, creates a more intimate atmosphere than might be
expected (bar food daily 12.30-9.45). Comfortably furnished modern
bedrooms are quite spacious, with bath and shower, phone,
satellite TV and tea/coffee-making facilities. Children are welcome:
there's an outdoor playground, and the Aquadome is nearby. Own
parking. Wheelchair accessible. No pets. 100 rooms (14 no-smoking,
1 for wheelchair users).

B&B £49 pps, single £69.

Closed 25 December.

Amex, MasterCard, Visa.

Directions: Town centre.

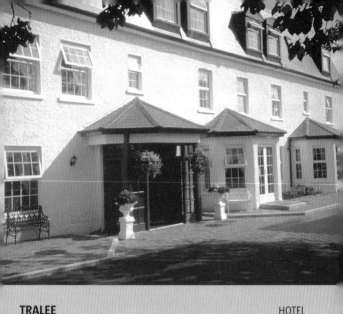

TRALEE   HOTEL

Ballygarry House Hotel

Killarney Road Tralee Co Kerry
Tel: 066 712 3322 Fax: 066 712 3322
email: ballygarry@eircom.net

Recently renovated and upgraded to a high standard, this pleasant roadside hotel on the outskirts of Tralee presents a neat face to arriving guests and also has extensive landscaped gardens. The furnishing style is traditional with occasional contemporary twists and very pleasing to the eye: warm colours, notably in oriental rugs used on wooden floors, create a welcoming atmosphere in public areas and darkwood furniture in bedrooms is used to effect against contrasting furnishings and pale walls. There's a pleasantly old-fashioned bar (food served 11am-9pm Monday-Saturday) and an elegant restaurant, The Riverside, where head chef Paudie Kerins presents internationally influenced menus based on local produce, as in Ring of Kerry salmon with poached leeks & lemongrass cream; lobster, sole and local meats feature This is an appealing hotel and moderately priced. Special breaks available. Children welcome. No pets. 30 rooms (1 for disabled). Lift. *New accommodation to include junior suites and executive rooms will open in early summer 2001.

B&B £40 pps, ss £40, sc 12.5%.

Closed 22-26 December.

Amex, Mastercard, Visa.

Directions: 1 mile outside Tralee town, on the Killarney road.

TRALEE, AT ARDFERT   GUESTHOUSE

Barrow Guest House

West Ardfert Tralee Co Kerry
Tel: 066 713 6437 Fax: 066 713 6402
email: infor@barrowhouse.com

This recently renovated guesthouse is in a stunning shoreside
position on Barrow Harbour and dates back to 1723. It was once
home to the Knight of Kerry and has largely retained its unique
tranquil setting and unspoilt views: the front bedrooms and public
rooms, which include a period drawing room and a breakfast room,
where both buffet and hot breakfasts are served, all have wonderful
views across water to the Slieve Mish Mountains and Dingle
peninsula. Bedrooms are spacious and extremely comfortable, with
orthopaedic beds, phone, satellliteTV, tea/coffee facilities and
lovely bathrooms, some with jacuzzi baths; everything has has been
completed to a very high standard and the atmosphere is in some
ways more like a hotel than a country house. Angling and golf are
major attractions - the Arnold Palmer designed Tralee Golf Club is
next door and Killarney, Ballybunion and Waterville within range.
Evening meals are not provided, but good restaurants nearby
include The Tankard and The Oyster Tavern. Some rooms are in an
adjacent courtyard. 9 rooms (1 suite; all no-smoking).

B&B £45 pps, single £65

Closed 20 December-14 February.

MasterCard, Visa.

Directions: Take the R558 and follow signs for Tralee Golf Club.

TRALEE   HOTEL

The Brandon Hotel

Princes Street Tralee Co Kerry
Tel: 066 712 3333 Fax: 066 712 5019

Very near the famous Siamsa Tire folk theatre, and close to the Aquadome, Tralee's largest hotel is attractively located on a wide tree-lined street and overlooks a park. It is also very convenient to the shopping and cultural areas of the town - and is at the heart of local activities throughout the area. Spacious public areas are impressive - the tone is set in the large foyer - and a wide range of accommodation is offered. Deluxe rooms at the top of the hotel are very large and luxurious and, while some other bedrooms are on the small side, all have been recently refurbished and have direct-dial phone, radio and TV (no tea/coffee-making facilities) and tiled bathrooms. There's a well-equipped leisure centre with swimming pool, sauna and steam room - and also good banqueting/conference facilities.

B&B from £35 pps

Closed 22-29 December.

Amex, Diners, MasterCard, Visa.

Directions: Town centre

Castlemorris House

Ballymullen, Tralee, Co Kerry.
Tel: 066 718 0060   Fax: 066 712 8007
email: castlemorris@eircom.net

Mary and Paddy Barry's attractive creeper-clad house dates back to 1790 and makes a lovely place to stay. It has the friendly atmosphere of a family home and good cooking includes home baking - guests get to sample that from an early stage as they are greeted with a complimentary afternoon tea in front of the drawing room fire on arrival. Bedrooms are spacious and well-furnished for comfort with style. Breakfast is a speciality and evening meals are available if you remember to book before noon - an appealing menu with two choices on each course is offered: starters like garlic sausage salad with tomato dressing or homemade seafood mousses and main courses such roast stuffed loin of pork with Madeira sauce or ovenbaked salmon en croûte are typical. Garden. Children over 10 welcome. Pets allowed by arrangement. 6 rooms (4 shower only).

B&B £35 pps, single £45.

Open all year.

Amex, MasterCard, Visa.

Directions: On the edge of Tralee town, left off N21 signed Dingle; 1/2 mile to T-junction, take a right turn - the house is on the right.

TRALEE   HOTEL

Grand Hotel

Denny Street Tralee Co Kerry
Tel: 066 712 1499 Fax: 066 712 2877
email: info@grandhoteltralee.com

Old world charm is the key characteristic of this family-owned hotel
in the heart of Tralee. Established in 1928, its furnishing style lives
up to its name with mahogany panelling and ornate plasterwork
creating the kind of ambience that suits town centre hotels of this
vintage. The forty four bedrooms offer moderately priced
accommodation with bath or shower, direct dial phones, multi-
channel television, hair dryers and tea/coffee making
facilities.Although the hotel does not have on-site leisure amenities,
residents have free use of the gym at Tralee Fitness Centre, 30%
discount on green fees at Tralee Golf Club and reduced admission to
the Aquadome. The real heart of the hotel is the characterful
Pikeman Bar - its bow-fronted window is promising from the street
and an open fireplace, dark mahogany and gleaming bar give it
great presence and it is held in great affection locally. Renowned for
atmosphere, it's a popular meeting place, with bar food served all
day (to 9.30 pm) and traditional music sessions with local musicians
in the evening.

B&B from £30 pps.

Closed 24-27 December

Amex, MasterCard, Visa.

Directions: Town centre.

Meadowlands Hotel

Oakpark, Tralee, Co Kerry
Tel: 066 718 0444   Fax: 066 718 0964
email: meadowlands@iol.ie

This fine hotel set quietly in landscaped gardens is just two years old and already the high quality of design, materials and workmanship, together with caring service from well-trained staff, is ensuring its position as one of Tralee's leading hotels. Stylish, well-designed bedrooms are spacious and comfortable, with striking decor; suites have jacuzzis and queen size beds, one a four-poster. All have individually controlled air conditioning and heating, multi-channel television, direct dial phones, tea/coffee-making facilities and trouser press with ironing board. The proprietor, Paddy O'Mahony, operates his own fishing boats, ensuring that seafood served in the restaurant "An Pota Stoir", is on the plate within hours of landing; head chef John O'Leary is fast gaining a reputation for imaginative menus and sound cooking, especially seafood - and the decor is appropriately nautical. The hotel bar, "Johnny Franks", offers informal fare such as home-made fish cakes and Dingle seafood platter, 12.30-9pm daily - and regularly features live music. Children welcome. Wheelchair accessible. Lift. No pets. 30 rooms (3 suites, 2 for wheelchair users).

B&B £60 pps, single £80.

Closed 24-26 December.

MasterCard, Visa.

Directions: 1 km. From Tralee town centre on the N69.

Fenit Harbour, nearby, is a fine leisure amenity for Tralee and source of fresh seafood for the area's pubs and restaurants

TRALEE   BAR/RESTAURANT

Oyster Tavern

The Spa Tralee Co Kerry
Tel: 066 713 6102 Fax: 066 713 6047

Heading out from Tralee along the shore road to Fenit, this large well-maintained bar and restaurant presents a neat face to arriving guests and has plenty of space around it for private parking and seating on sunny days. Jim McGrath, who has been owner-manager for 22 years, has achieved and maintained high standards of food and service here over a long period of time, earning a loyal local following, including the Tralee horse-racing set - famous patrons have included the great Frankie Dettori whose photograph hangs in the bar. The restaurant, which is delightfully informal and blends effortlessly into the bar, looks across Tralee Bay to the Slieve Mish Mountains and, although not on the sea side of the road, the hillside location allows lovely uninterrupted views on clear days. Menus are well-balanced and moderately priced - and given the location, it will come as no surprise to learn that seafood is a speciality. Sunday lunch is especially good value and very popular. Open 10.30am -11pm, lunch and dinner served daily.

Closed 25 December, Good Friday.

Diners, MasterCard, Visa.

Directions: 4 miles outside Tralee, on the Fenit road.

TRALEE   RESTAURANT

Restaurant Uno

14 Princes Street Tralee Co Kerry
Tel: 066 718 1950 Fax: 066 718 1951

Just across the road from the town park, Maeve Duff's unusual
restaurant is in several areas, each with a different personality: a
cosy front room doubles as reception and opens into a second high-
ceilinged room which is brightly lit and more modern in style, with
yet another seating area in a balcony area above it. It has built up
a great following since she took over these premises in 1999 and
menus favour the contemporary side of the restaurant's psyche,
with a leaning toward Cal-Ital and global influences plus a
seasoning of more traditional dishes - Chinese duck spring roll with
sweet chilli dip is a typical starter and main courses might include
Thai red chicken, vegetable curry with coconut rice & poppadums or
home-made burgers and steaks, all reasonably priced. Atmosphere,
friendly service and good value make this a popular venue. Not
suitable for children after 8 pm. No smoking area. Lunch Monday-
Saturday12.30-2.15, Dinner daily 5.30-10 (Sunday from 4); à la carte.

Closed Sunday Lunch; 1 week early January.

Amex, Diners, MasterCard, Visa.

Directions: Next to the Brandon Hotel.

TRALEE, AT FENIT   PUB/RESTAURANT

The Tankard

Kilfenora Fenit Co Kerry
Tel: 066 713 6164 Fax: 066 713 6516

Mary and Jerry O'Sullivan's brightly painted pub and restaurant on
the seaward side of the road has earned a great reputation,
especially for seafood cooking, which can be exceptional. An
imaginative bar menu is available from lunchtime to late evening (1-
9) serving the likes of "smokeys", boxty and warm chicken salad
seafood. While bar menus give a passing nod to current trends, the
restaurant style is quite traditional and beyond fashion - simple
well-cooked food, based on the finest of local ingredients with
excellent saucing and unfussy presentation makes a refreshing
change from the ubiquitous 'world cuisine'. Although most famous
for seafood there's quite a wide choice, especially steaks in various
guises, duckling, Kerry lamb and some strong vegetarian options.
There are sea and mountain views from the restaurant, which has
recently been extended and opened out to make the most of its
location, with a patio area and a path down to the sea. Dinner daily
6-10, set menus from £16, also à la carte; Lunch Sunday only 12.30-
2, Set Sunday Lunch £12.95. Closed 25 December & Good Friday.

Amex, Diners, MasterCard, Visa

Directions: From Tralee, 5 miles out on the Fenit road, beyond the
Spa.

TRALEE, AT FENIT BAR/RESTAURANT/ACCOMMODATION

West End Bar

Fenit Tralee Co Kerry
Tel: 066 713 6246

The O'Keeffes' family-run pub is exactly seven minutes walk from the marina. Good food is available in both the bar and the restaurant, which is earning a sound reputation in the area and has recently been extended to include a conservatory. Head chef Bryan O'Keeffe's style is "classic French with Irish popular cuisine", with seafood and meats billed equally as specialities. Expect starters ranging from Atlantic fisherman's chowder with brown bread, through local 'Cromane' mussels with bayleaves, garlic & cream, to egg mayonnaise and deep-fried 'Roulet Brie' pieces. Main courses include old favourites - sirloin steak, half roast duckling, rack of lamb - and a range of seafood dishes including sole on the bone (with lemon butter) and turbot ((steam-baked, with a leek & martini sauce) at very reasonable prices. Simple, inexpensive accommodation is offered in ten en-suite rooms Bar/restaurant Meals 5.30-9.30 daily in summer. A la carte. Phone ahead to check food service off-season.

B&B £20, no single supplement

Bar closed 25 December & Good Friday.

MasterCard, Visa.

Directions: 8 miles from Tralee; on the corner as you turn down to the marina.

Photo - Waterville Golf Links

Waterville

Waterville is based on golf and fish. At first glance, it seems to be little more than a row of houses on the shores of beautiful Ballinskelligs Bay. So you might well ask, what on earth is Waterville for? But then you discover that, right on the back of the village, there's the large expanse of Lough Currane, a splendid lake only 19ft above sea level, and providing some extraordinarily good fishing.

And then, you get to hear of the golf. This is golf for serious golfers. Waterville Golf Course is for heroes and heroines - it's a massive championship links set at a challenging par 74.

Thus Waterville has the absorbing attraction of a place which attracts specialist and dedicated visitors. Among those visitors, there have been some very famous people. And between the lot of them, they're a remarkably eclectic mix, all of which adds to the entertainment. So even if you're not a golfer or an angler, you'll find Waterville an intriguing little place, and hospitable with it.

Butler Arms Hotel

Waterville Co Kerry

Tel: 066 947 4144 Fax: 066 947 4520

Like many hotels which have been owner-run for several generations Peter and Mary Huggards' famous seafront hotel has established a special reputation for its homely atmosphere and good service. It makes an ideal holiday location, with many activities close by: Waterville's championship golf links are just a mile away and the area is also renowned for salmon and seatrout fishing, bird-watching, horseriding and walking as well as sandy beaches. Well-maintained public areas, including a well-appointed restaurant specialising in local seafood, two sitting rooms, a sun lounge and a cocktail bar, are all spacious and comfortably furnished, while the beamed Fisherman's Bar provides a livelier atmosphere. Bedrooms vary from distinctly non-standard rooms in the old part of the hotel (which many regular guests request) to smartly decorated rooms with neat en-suite bathrooms and uninterrupted sea views in a wing constructed in the early '90s. Off season value breaks; shooting parties (woodcock, snipe) November-January. Garden; tennis. Snooker. Wheelchair accessible. Own parking. Children welcome. Lift. 30 rooms (2 suites).

B&B £70 pps, single £95.

Closed mid October-mid April.

Amex, Diners, MasterCard, Visa.

Directions: N70, 50 miles SouthWest of Killarney in centre of village.

THE MAGIC OF
Kerry

DRAÍOCHT CHIARRAÍ
Spectacular scenery and hospitable people...
an ideal place to live, work or visit

**KERRY COUNTY COUNCIL
PROTECTING THE ENVIRONMENT**

Ag Caomhnú Timpeallacht Chiarraí

Index

i tourist information

Cead Mile Fáilte
- Cork/Kerry Tourism and
Shannon Development extend a very warm
welcome to County Kerry.

Kerry, which is better known as the 'Kingdom', is world famous for its scenery, facilities, hospitality and its food. Dining in Kerry is a unique experience due mainly to the quality of the ingredients and the creativity of its preparation. Dishes such as Kerry Lambs and the vast array of freshly caught seafood are just some of the delicacies available.

The quality of the welcome from Kerry's top class accommodation providers is world renowned. Why not take the time to explore the vast range of dining and accommodation options available in this guide?

Please feel free to use the services available from our network of Tourism Offices and Tourism Information Points which will help you book accommodation and advise on visitor facilities. Bureau de Change is also available. Enjoy your stay.

tourist offices

Detailed information on Kerry available in the 'Kerry Guide' and accommodation booking/information through your Tourist Office. The international telephone access code for Ireland is: **353**

Cork/Kerry Tourism - **www.ireland.travel.ie**
Shannon Development - **www.shannon-dev.ie**

tourist information offices

Cahersiveen	066 947 2589	June - Sep.
Dingle	066 915 1188 / 066 915 1241	March -Oct.
Kenmare	064 41233	April - Sep.
Killarney	064 31633 / Fax 064 34506	All Year
Listowel	068 22590	May - Sep.
Tralee	066 712 1288 / Fax 066 712 1700	All Year
Waterville	066 9474646	June - Sep.

tourist information points

Ballybunion	(Main Street)	068 27711
Castleisland	(The Island Centre, Main Street)	066 947 2676
Cloghane	(Cloghane)	066 713 8277
Kells	(Pat's Craft Shop)	066 947 7601
Killorglin	(Fax 066 9761825)	066 976 1451
Tarbert	(Bridewell)	068 36500

CORK KERRY TOURISM
The Special Rates South

SHANNON DEVELOPMENT